Broken by Addiction

MW00436829

Blessed by God

A Woman's Path
to Sustained Recovery

PENNY MARY HAUSER, MSN

Liguori
LIGUORI, MISSOURI

To Joe, who continues to open my eyes, my ears,
and my life to the promises of God.

Imprimi Potest:
Thomas D. Picton, C.Ss.R.
Provincial, Denver Province
The Redemptorists

Published by Liguori Publications
Liguori, Missouri 63057
To order, call 800-325-9521
www.liguori.org

Copyright © 2010 Penny Mary Hauser

All rights reserved. No part of this book may be reproduced, stored in a re-
trieval system, or transmitted without the prior written permission of Liguori
Publications.

Library of Congress Cataloging-in-Publication Data
Hauser, Penny Mary.
    Broken by addiction, blessed by God / Penny Mary Hauser. — 1st ed.
      p. cm.
    ISBN 978-0-7648-1893-6
    1. Addicts—Religious life. 2. Christian women—Substance use. 3.
Substance abuse—Religious aspects—Christianity. I. Title.

    BV4596.A24H38 2010
    248.8'629082—dc22

                                          2009048266

Liguori Publications, a nonprofit corporation, is an apostolate of the
Redemptorists. To learn more about the Redemptorists, visit Redemptorists.
com.

Printed in the United States of America
14 13 12 11 10   5 4 3 2 1
First edition

Contents

Acknowledgments

It is with great pleasure and deep gratitude that I wish to thank so many people who helped form my thinking in the development and writing of this book.

First to my family—Joe, my husband, to whom this book is dedicated; to my precious sons, Jack and Joe, and their families; and to my daughter, Merry Pat, whose spirit remains with me every day.

To Mom and Dad for their gift of faith.

To "Nancy," who gave the gift of trust, and to all the women with whom we laughed and cried and learned.

To the Stone Center for its research, writings, and "Work in Progress," which framed much of my thought about women's uniqueness.

To the therapists who set me on the path—Sandy Dautch and Tom Burns.

To Em Olivia Bevis, teacher and friend, whose powerful words of encouragement linger as inspiring messages. To Carol J. Farran, professor and mentor, who helped with my exploration of women and anger.

To friends and family who have been supporters and cheerleaders and walked with me through the mountains and valleys: Janet Marshall, Gene Olsen, Helen Matthews, Janace Cole, Lee Schmidt, Mary Smillie, Carol Fernier, Sherry Rhynard, Judy Warriner-Walke, Janet Field, Betty Lord, Carolyn Bayer Hauser, and Miriam Hauser.

To Ann Bavry for her time, her review, her enthusiasm, and her suggestions.

To Steve Beste and Tim Hauser for "technical support."

To Deborah Meister, Liguori editor, for her "passionate pitch" and warm reassurances.

And to Karen Speerstra, whose personal and professional skills, talents, and flair have accompanied this project from conception to delivery. A friend is someone who doesn't ask why I did a thing, only what do we need to do now that I've done it! That is Karen.

Introduction

For twenty years I have had the privilege of working with women who have been moving within recovery—recovery from substance abuse and many other demons. And over the years I have seen so many women, just as I have seen myself, struggling with relapse. What are we missing? What makes this so difficult? Why are there so many of us who don't seem to "get it" but keep on wanting "it" and working toward "it"? Is the "it" just abstaining from drinking or drugging or shopping or sex or bingeing? Or is "it" something more?

Though the process of recovery from addiction is never easy, some women seem to move through the journey with less pain than others. Why? What makes the difference? The chapters of this book explore some of the concerns and issues that women in recovery tell us are unique to them as women. It also looks at ways to approach these issues using perspectives that touch the truth of who we are.

Women share their stories, because that's what we women do best. Doing so helps us make sense of the chaos surrounding our lives. You'll hear many women's stories here, as well as my own. These stories talk about how we identified that we had an addiction, how we began to work on staying away from our drug of choice or addictive behaviors, how we explored the life issues that kept tripping us up in our recovery, and how we began to explore a relationship with God as central to sustained recovery. This is the process of recovery. The stories help us move together in recovery. Some of the stories are painful, horrific, and tragic. Some are humorous. All "tell it like it was" for these women, before they named the addiction, how they figured "it" out, and how they, as women, stumbled or danced in recovery. It is also about how "happily ever after" is working out—or not.

AN EPIDEMIC OF ADDICTION—THE DISEASE

Researchers and therapists have examined many different treatment programs and different therapeutic approaches in an attempt to find out what "works." However, the epidemic of addiction continues to rage for women of all ages, races, and socioeconomic levels. The Cleveland Clinic's recent statistics report that more than four million U.S. women abuse drugs or alcohol (see References). That's a lot of us!

What is going on?

Because most of the past research has been done in men, could it be that we are missing some of the unique aspects the disease of addiction has for women? Unique aspects of how we enter the disease of addiction and unique aspects of how we recover? One of the more useful variables in women's recovery, which has been recognized by some health professionals over the past fifteen to twenty years, is the need for a specialized, gender-specific approach. In this book we explore the "what" and the "why" of gender-focused recovery. Addiction and recovery issues may be similar for men and women, but the ways women experience, talk, and think about them are quite different. Therefore, significant perspectives of recovery related to women need to be approached in different ways—a beginning point is to clarify our language, and another is to look at the most frequently cited barrier to entering recovery: the stigma.

CLARIFYING OUR LANGUAGE

Because the focus of this book is on addiction, we need to attempt to define that somewhat elusive term. The Harvard Health Publications' (see References) clinical definition of addiction is frequently used in the health care field. Their definition includes the "four C's" and can be helpful for starters:

- We engage in destructive behaviors that are stimulated by sensations that range from Craving to Compulsion.
- We continue to use drugs/alcohol even when there are very negative Consequences.
- And, ultimately, we lose Control.

Women understand these C's very clearly when thinking about behaviors that need to change.

Three areas to think about that make the four C's personal:

1. *Can I no longer predict what will happen when I use, drink, drug, gamble, or whatever?* (On a given occasion does the craving lead me to use more/drink more [compulsion] than I told myself I would?)
2. *Is it getting in the way of who I want to be and how I want to lead my life?* (Have I lost important things in my life because of my addiction? Am I at risk of losing important things? Have I behaved in ways that embarrass me when I think of them?)
3. *Does it cause me to pull away from God?* (Are there times I get scared? Do I tell myself I don't care? Do I tell myself God is not important to the way I want to live?)

Our struggles as women are not limited just to the demons of substance abuse. We struggle with depression, anxiety disorders, eating disorders, obesity, shopping, smoking, gambling, and sexual behavior. Sometimes we couple these demons with mood-altering substances, and sometimes they appear without the substance. If you are in search of ways to think differently about any demon and wish to expand your thinking about recovery to include your relationships and spiritual growth, we are delighted you are here.

WHAT IS STIGMA?

Earlier we said the greatest barrier to entering recovery is the stigma of being an addict. When a woman speaks of being an alcoholic or addict, she experiences a deep *stigma*—a stain, a shame. *Stigma* makes a mark and stains our good reputation. *Disgraceful*. We are branded with "shame" and "embarrassment." It's difficult to admit we are addicts. Friends, family, and society look down on a woman who has a disease of addiction. A man who uses drugs or gets drunk is often seen as "one of the guys." A woman who is an addict is "coarse, a weak slut, a tramp." This stigma is the greatest barrier to a woman acknowledging the disease and entering recovery.

In this book we expand the use of the word *stigma*. Using the first letters of particular words as the issues of recovery, we form the acronym of STIGMA. These particular words identify and explore issues of recovery embedded in the stories of recovering women. Exploring these issues helps name the pain and deal with the shame.

The particular words that name the issues of women's recovery and the chapter titles are as follows:

S identifies our negative Self-image.

T stands for the Traditional roles we see as limiting our choices.

I points out how Ineffective our communication usually is.

G represents our intense Grief and loss and our guilt and shame.

M means all the Medical issues surrounding addiction.

A is for the Anger and abuse that particularly surrounds women caught in an addiction and recovery cycle.

STIGMA

Each of these STIGMA issues is explored in a separate chapter, and each is examined in a framework of three interacting themes that guide the progressive stages of recovery:

1. The identification of the issues from our personal and cultural experiences.
2. The work of recovery in which we change some of our ways of doing and thinking. We explore the unique impact and power of women's *relational development* on those issues.
3. The peace that comes in placing the issues and work within one's *relationship with God*.

In this framework, you are encouraged to examine your own story, to identify areas of pain and of healing in your own life, and to imagine openly how things might be different. In each chapter these themes are developed in progressive stages. You will be encouraged to *name* your story and issues, *transform* your story using the power of relationships, and *sustain* the peace of recovery. What does all this mean? *It means we work on the STIGMA issues of recovery using the three themes to guide our thinking, and we develop that work within the recovery process.*

A bit more about the three interacting themes:

1. Issues of recovery

During my early years of clinical practice I listened to numerous women's stories related to addiction, recovery, and other mental health and life challenges. Consistent subjects, the STIGMA issues, began to emerge. These six broad subjects or issues form the skeletal structure and chapter titles of this book. Each will explore the power we give the issues, their impact on addiction, our vulnerability to relapse, and our recovery.

You will hear how various women identified issues that led to and kept them trapped in their addictions. Later in each chapter, their voices reveal how they moved through those issues into making recovery decisions and into a sustained recovery. These ideas are not meant to be a prescription for treatment and recovery. Rather, they are offered as a guide to help you discover ways the issues of STIGMA might have an impact on you in your journey into recovery.

2. Healthy relationships strengthen recovery

Once we acknowledge we have this disease of addiction, learning to live in connection, acceptance, and peace comes in reframing some of our patterns of thinking and some of our patterns of behavior. We learn to live in relationship—relationship with ourselves, with our families and friends, and with God. A discussion of relationships supports every part of this book.

The Stone Center at Wellesley College in Boston has done a great deal of research in "self-in-relation" or "women's relational theory." Its work states that as women we measure our growth and well-being through relationships that are mutually strengthening and valued. Its model of women's growth says involvement in healthy relationships creates a sense of energy, an understanding of oneself and others, a sense of self-worth, and an interest in further connection. These connections also profoundly affect a woman's conflicts and crises. We will make use of the Stone Center's findings to consider the personal growth needed in recovery—the growth connected with our feelings, challenges, and decisions as we approach and work through the issues and tasks of recovery.

3. Exploring recovery in a relationship with God.

Remember, only a clear head can really examine the issues, complete the tasks, and begin to understand that recovery hinges in large part on another vital relationship—our relationship with God. The joy begins when we understand that God is always in the struggle with us, holding us—no matter what! Isn't that an incredible feeling? Emmanuel—God with us! Not just at Christmas, but every minute of every day—days we spend in joyous recovery and especially days when the challenge is painful.

PROCESS OF RECOVERY

"I am in the process of recovery." This is a key sentence. Say it again: "I am in the process of recovery." It may be long and painful, and you may likely have some stumbles, but you are on the path.

Generally accepted definitions of *recovery* seem extremely benign when applied to women and addiction. Dictionary definitions imply recovery as a return to some "normal" condition after an illness. This hardly speaks to the struggles, pain, and joy that accompany the recovery we are talking about here. Professional and self-help definitions generally equate recovery with abstinence. Often a professional definition of recovery includes the premise of a *total abolition* of drinking (drug) problems.

However, I have come to believe that a definition of recovery from addiction needs to acknowledge the *process of recovery*. Recovery takes a long time, is not a straight line, and usually has many starts and stops.

Addiction is really like a tiger creeping along in the tall grass next to us. We get into trouble if we ignore it, pretend it's tamed, act as if it's on a leash, or maybe even pet it. Then when we least expect it, the addiction-tiger rises up and bites us "on the ass," as a good friend puts it. For a lot of us in the process of recovery, we believe we are making progress. We acknowledge our issues, and we think it's all working fine. It's safe to walk through tall grass (risky people, places, things). But then it growls. If we ignore it, the tiger leaps!

Once that tiger leaps, we are in the throes of relapse. *Relapse* feels like such a failure. We get discouraged. We think, "I can't start again....It's useless....I have to pick up a new chip....I can't walk into that meeting." This is all part of the stigma of addiction, as well as part of the creative challenge of recovery. But other people with chronic illnesses don't feel that they are a failure when their disease recurs. People with diabetes don't hang their heads when their sugar levels rise or fall. They look at their diets, or stress, or exercise, and they make adjustments. They consult with health experts and may decide to attend an educational support group. They know recovery means continually learning how to live daily with their disease.

We, too, need to learn to live with the disease. And once we acknowledge that our addiction keeps us from being who we want to be, we are in recovery. If we use addictive substances or addictive behaviors again, we have not *failed*. We definitely need to examine the issues (STIGMA), consult with experts (counselors/medical), and get self-help (sponsors). We learn to live with our disease. We *can* make changes in how we think and what we do. And, perhaps most important, we will learn to live with our recovery through connection, acceptance, and peace.

As we talk about the process of recovery in this book, the individual chapters examine how each of these STIGMA issues make themselves known and felt (*name*), how we address the issues in recovery particularly with the support of healthy relationships (*transform*), and how we move into the peace of long-term recovery (*sustain*). These terms point toward the movement, the courage, the creativity, and the joy that are recovery.

FROM BROKEN BY ADDICTION TO BLESSED BY GOD

There are no specific time frames for these stages, and I believe each of us works on the STIGMA issues again and again. They spiral through our lives over and over. Each time that we examine these various issues and stages, we encounter them with expanding depth and breadth. This is how the journey of recovery progresses. Each time that we consider the issues and work on the tasks, we diminish the hold the negative stigma has on us. In each stage we will think about where we are in our spiritual growth and in our relationship with God and his divine power. We become both more delicate and more forceful as we gain a trust in ourselves, a trust in others, and a trust in his promises. At the beginning of this journey there is often a glimpse of joy and peace.

How do we make that initial joy last? Where does the peace of long-term recovery come from? If we, as women, can risk an exploration of our spiritual core, of God, and of how God fits into our recovery, then maybe we can begin to find that sense of peace and joy that leads to lasting recovery. Just maybe we will begin to recognize ourselves as deeply forgiven, loved, and blessed.

Will you be open to this kind of exploration and conversation? I invite you to stop and think and feel as we talk. It's your path. You make your own choices. And you are not alone!

CHAPTER 1

S: Self-image

*W*hat makes you think you need to change something in your life?

You've tried this before. What's going to be different this time?

Are you willing to look at this from a new angle?

Many women asked these questions, told their own stories, and identified the themes and recovery stages that form the outline of this book. We talked, we laughed, and we cried. We had "umm's" and "aha's." We shared our hopes, our dreams, and our various successes and setbacks. Each story you read here is rich with the courage of wanting life to be different.

Although these are the stories of many women, one woman illuminates many of the STIGMA issues that we identified in the Introduction and that we will discuss as the focus of each chapter. We will call her Nancy, and her story will lead our way.

Nancy's life story, including her addictions and her journey of recovery, has it all—all the STIGMA issues with her _S_elf-image, _T_raditional roles, _I_neffective communication, _G_rief/loss: guilt/ shame, _M_edical aspects, and _A_nger/abuse. Nancy's story takes shape within her relationships of family and friends. And miraculously, her long-term, ongoing recovery is ultimately about her relationship with God.

NANCY'S STORY

As Nancy remembers it, her childhood was a nightmare. It was filled with memories of endless abuse. She was physically abused by both parents, sexually abused by her father and brother, and deprived of any demonstration of love or warmth or tenderness.

To escape from an unsafe home and a destructive family, she married at sixteen. And as so often happens, Nancy's nightmare continued because she married a man who beat her as her sons hid in their bedrooms. Nancy became a plumber. She worked by herself. It was a dirty job. It was hard work. She worked for low wages, and she was abused by her employer. Then her favorite son committed suicide.

Nancy began drinking when she was eight and started smoking marijuana at fourteen. A few years ago she responded to the call of crack cocaine. She said the chemicals numbed her deep pain.

One day Nancy went on a drinking binge and lost her van. "The whole f*****g van," she said, "I lost the whole f*****g van. That's when I knew it was time to do something."

Nancy was admitted to treatment for chemical dependency—first to inpatient, then intensive outpatient, then longer-term outpatient. I'd like to say that Nancy's recovery has been possible through a dynamic women's program. It has not. Her individual work, group work, and counseling relationships have held her safely and honored her gender-specific issues. She has had a long-term relationship with a pastoral counselor. They have both been willing to share their conversations with me.

Nancy's recovery was a core piece of the development of this work. Her honesty and effort showed me how many of these pieces fit together. Her recovery has had its share of stumbles. But each time, Nancy has been willing to go back to the issues and look at where the pain still holds her. Each time, she has been willing to push a little further, dig a bit deeper, and risk a bit more. Nancy has taught me how these STIGMA issues affected her addiction and her recovery and how her addiction and her recovery were for her as a woman.

You may feel that some struggles and successes in Nancy's story are identical with your experience. Other issues may have little to do with your story of addiction or recovery or demons. I simply encourage you to be open to Nancy's shared experience. Let it roll around a little in your mind and in your heart and see whether anything happens. Let's first look at Nancy's self-image.

Self-image

Self-image, self-esteem, self-concept, and self-worth are all terms to define how we feel about ourselves. Most psychological theories claim that we develop this sense of self in our earliest years from parents, teachers, and adults close to us. What these important people say we are often becomes who we believe we really are. We hear their voices ringing in our minds every day for the rest of our lives.

Generation after generation the things adults around us say, their attitudes and beliefs, imprint our souls. We inherit their viewpoints and use them to make choices. We also take note of their actions and often mirror them in our own adult lives. From those choices and actions we witness, we live the consequences we call our lives.

As we closely watch and absorb the beliefs and actions of the adults close to us, we learn how to deal with the world. For example, if our relationship with our parents is nurturing and predictable, we tend to see the world as trustworthy. If our parents see the world as fair, we see the world as fair. Was the message you heard at home something like, "Life can be hard but if we love one another we can make it more meaningful"?

On the other hand, if our parents see the world as a threat or unfair, then we also learn to believe we live in a threatening, unfair world. "Don't trust anybody! They're all out to cheat you." If this is what our parents repeatedly told us, then it becomes difficult for us to trust.

What our parents tell us and how they behave also affects how we feel about ourselves. Perhaps they used direct messages such as "You're bright and can be anything you want to be" or "You're so stupid. How can you even think that?" Children also absorb more indirect but nevertheless powerful messages. If her mother is depressed or angry, a little girl might think to herself, "What did I do? Am I responsible for her sadness? How can I make her happy?"

We draw our conclusions about how to deal with the world and with our precious selves by how we understand our parents' behavior and attitudes. Of course, external forces such as illness, poverty, or world events also play a powerful role in what shapes us, but the strongest influence on who we come to believe we are, our self-image, stems from our relationship with our parents.

Self-image and Relationships

The Stone Center at Wellesley College (see References) has done helpful work on the subject of how we develop as women. Its founding theory states that the primary way a woman defines who she is, her self-image, comes from her relationship with her mother. As a girl she spends much time with her mother. She watches, listens, and learns how to be a girl and, eventually, how to be a woman. She pulls the positive and the negative into her own self-image. As she watches her mother, the daughter often develops a mothering identity, a care-giving relationship. She "mothers" her dolls as her mother mothers. Very early, girls show the need to take care of the important relationships in their lives. The daughter helps in household tasks but might also take on the role of helping mother feel less sad, depressed, or angry.

A girl's self-image is based on her early conviction that she is in a loving and caring relationship and her "job" is to nurture that relationship. That works out very well for us most of the time. It feels good. It feels right. However, this becomes problematic when it is the *only* way a woman can be in relationship. When the caretaker role becomes the exclusive role of the woman, she feels trapped. When she is the only caretaker in the relationship and it is going badly, she can begin to believe she is a failure as wife, mother, and partner. The good news is that a broken, painful relationship can be an impetus for change. Most of the women I have worked with acknowledge that it was their broken relationships and their destroyed self-image around those relationships that forced them to look seriously at their addictions.

What does it mean in our addiction when we begin to recognize (*name*) that our relationships are deteriorating? The powerful disease of addiction usually causes us to blame everyone and everything outside of ourselves. But when we begin to notice that the people we love most are being negatively affected by the addiction, we often hear the wake-up call. For some women this wake-up call comes in the form of words or behaviors of their children.

Carol tells of one morning when she could not get her head off the pillow. Her four-year-old son came into her room and asked, "What's wrong, Mommy? Don't you got no more Percocet? You want some cereal?" At that moment, she made the decision something had to change. He knew. Her son knew she depended on the pills. Carol could no longer say, "This doesn't touch my son."

Marie recalls telling the kids she was going out to get bread or school supplies, and then she would stop for "just one." Hours later she would return home to children asleep on the sofa, the peanut butter jar open, and no homework done.

One day I asked Joanne, a secretary in our office, how she got the bruises on her arms. She said, "I get crazy when I drink. My husband has to restrain me." Later, she told me her son is now in therapy. "I tell him it isn't his fault but he doesn't believe me. He cries and begs me not to drink." The effects of our addictions cause pain at our core and at the core of those we love most, especially our children.

The disease progresses, relationships deteriorate, and isolation increases. That is what addiction does. When a man's disease progresses, he often spends more time in the bars and out with the boys, but, when a woman's disease progresses, she often hides.

The stories women tell are similar no matter their age or background. A beautiful young woman told me people thought she could hold her liquor and was the life of the party. As her disease progressed she'd go to the bars, and friends would cheer her along as she downed tequila shots. By the end of the evening, she was so drunk no one wanted her around. She began to stay home and drink.

The wife of a very senior military officer said, "He goes to the parties. I stay home and take my bottle to bed. My son doesn't know. He just comes to the door and thinks I'm resting." All of us who grew up in alcoholic or substance-abusing homes know that's baloney! He knows!

How many times have I promised myself I would stop? How many times have I said, "I won't do that again. I won't drink/ use today"? And each time I fail, I tell myself I am a failure. I am weak. "How could I do that? I am a worthless piece of nothing!" I feel the self-loathing and the shame. All of these thoughts make us even more vulnerable.

So we deny and minimize. "I'm not that bad." This, however, leads to a profound distrust of our own self and increases our shame. Did you ever get up during the night and walk around in the dark desperately wondering, "What am I going to do about this?" You make a promise that tomorrow it will be different. You won't drink or use or binge. But by noon you're back at it again.

And the voice in your head tells you that repeated failures make you a failure.

Or maybe you do manage to string together a few days or a few weeks without the drugs. There is a beginning awareness that life *can* be different. Then there's a party or a crisis, and you're convinced you need the pill or booze. You can really handle it this time. And when you can't, you blame "them." It's *their* fault. But deep down, you tell yourself, "You broke the promise; you can't be trusted." We know how Nancy feels. She "lost the whole f*****g van!" What is it you've lost? The core of who you want to be? The strength of your family ties? The connection of your friendships? The woman, the mother, the wife your loved ones thought you were? What is your truth?

Disease Progresses

In addition to our early parental influence, the disease itself has an impact on our self-image. Like any disease, the disease of addiction has its own signs and symptoms. Just as a fever is an early sign of infection, denial is an early sign of the disease of addiction. We can deny we even have the disease, and denial allows us to be blind to its effects. Early in an infection or virus the fever is low and barely noticeable, but left untreated the fever can rise to the point that it destroys brain function. Early in addiction, denial of the disease allows us to convince ourselves things aren't so bad, and, therefore, we can't be so bad. But eventually the impact of the disease destroys everything around us—our relationships, our self-image, our values, our joy. The progression of the disease is devastating.

We must *name* the problem, *transform* our thinking and behavior, and *sustain* our recovery in a relationship with the divine presence in our lives.

NAME

In the denial we repeat the same phrases over and over. "It isn't that bad....I'm not that bad....I was just tired....He made me so angry....She's worse than I am....I'm under so much stress." But if we are lucky, there comes a time when denial doesn't work anymore. If we are not lucky, tragedy comes. A night of too many glasses of wine, driving through a stop sign, and a young man becomes paralyzed. An overdose of prescription drugs and we are in a coma. Too much coke and our heart stops. If we are lucky, or blessed, something or someone grabs our attention before the tragedy occurs.

Because of the nature of addiction, we rarely come to this great insight by ourselves. Maybe, like Nancy, we lost the van. Maybe we got a DUI. Maybe we were confronted at work. Maybe we used the gas money for cocaine. Maybe we stole. Maybe our husband yelled, "Damn it, not again!" But each time we said, "It really wasn't that bad. I can handle this. I won't let it happen again." The people we love let us hold them in a perpetual state of waiting and "what if," and we really do believe it won't happen again. We tell ourselves our relationships are safe.

I know I felt that way, as if I could keep control of my family and work relationships while I fell apart on the inside. But I was wrong. The first time I was confronted at work was the most humiliating day of my life. I had been the "good" girl, raised in an alcoholic home. I knew how to please people, make everything look "just fine." My drinking had increased during my early marriage as the opportunities increased: marriage to a military officer, parties with lots of alcohol, learning the relaxation and "fun" that came with a few drinks, years alone with young children while my husband served overseas and pursued his career. I could drink during those days and enjoy a buzz with no one noticing.

Finally, I decided to return to work. I had a college degree in nursing. With all the denial I could muster, I reasoned that if I worked a 3 to 11 PM shift, I would never drink before I went to work. But, of course, I was fooling myself. After about a year of being "good," I was having a glass of wine with lunch and ultimately a couple of belts of bourbon. And it got worse. At times I drove to work in a blackout. What on earth was I thinking?! How could I be responsible to take care of patients?! So it would get better for a few weeks. And then finally, one evening I was called into the director's office and confronted. They asked about my slurred speech. I said it was the blood pressure meds I was on. They asked about drinking. "No! You can take a blood test." (Isn't righteous indignation a hoot!) But I felt a shame deep in my core.

How could this happen to me? I am the one who has it together. And so I promised myself "never again." Several months later, it happened again. That is the nature of addiction. When I no longer can predict what will happen after I take the first drink or hit or drug, I am an addict. I was sent home that night. I cried all the way. I told my family my eyes were red and swollen because I'd had an allergic reaction to cleaning solution at the hospital. The lies, the denial, and the addiction continued. The humiliation became anger I directed toward myself. Several months later, my husband received orders for a transfer to another military base. I resigned the nursing position. The addiction told me a "geographic cure" would be the answer.

A Glimmer of Reality

Of course, the move was not a cure, and it took several more months for me to *name* the problem.

It is so scary to name the problem, because then we might have to do something—we might have to make some changes! Just thinking about it, just wishing, is not going to make it go away. We have to say the words, "I am an alcoholic, an addict"—stigma or not. The denial of the disease makes this so incredibly difficult. We have spent so much time lying to ourselves, telling ourselves we can control it.

But there is some good news here! Often the truth that we miss at this stage is the paradoxical power we gain once we acknowledge that we are powerless over the disease. We need a glimmer of this reality, of the power to be gained. Once we accept that we have the disease and have no control over the drink or drug or behavior, we gain power over our lives. I have lost control over alcohol/drugs, but I have regained power over my decisions. Isn't that incredible? We have choices!

We *can* do the "next right thing." And the next right thing is to connect with someone. We don't have to do this alone. We can find someone we can trust. It is important to go slowly in the beginning, but it is vital to begin. Perhaps there is a clergyperson or a doctor or nurse who might help find the beginning of the path. For instance, Jan talks of going to Mass on Ash Wednesday desperate to do something. After Mass she went to the priest's office, and, although he was putting on his jacket to go to lunch, she simply insisted he stay and talk with her. It turned out he knew another woman parishioner who was active in self-help and with Jan's permission arranged a telephone contact. It became one of her first steps on the journey.

Is there a friend who once talked with you about your addiction? Did she ask if she could help? Is there someone you know who is in recovery? Maybe you laughed when she told you she was in a program, and you said to yourself, "I'm glad I'm not that bad." Is there a doctor who might have some phone numbers? Is there a self-help group with daily or weekly meetings? Look it up in the phone book or on the Internet. Do they have a women's group? Is there a mental health group or clinic to give some guidance? Anyone who has "been there" knows how hard it is to pick up that phone for the first time. Almost all folks in self-help or therapists will encourage you to pick up the phone, but, if they've been there, they know it is one of the hardest things to do.

If nothing changes, nothing changes.

Little Choices—Loud Voices

And so we begin to make those little choices, such as making connections with people who can help. At this early stage, these choices are based in the here and now. One important choice related to our new self-image is to be more aware of those voices from the past, those messages in our head, the ones other people have given us about who we are. They come from long ago and from our own self-talk when the addiction was active. They can be loud and forceful. So we must begin the work to change how we respond to them. We learn to hear them as in the past, not in our new reality of recovery. We learn to do something different when we hear them now.

Take a moment to think about whom and what you hear when those voices speak. Name that person. Describe the words and write them down so they become real to you. Is the voice loving and affirming or a hurtful, frightening voice? Simply choose to bring that awareness into your thoughts. When Nancy drank or used and, even when she didn't, she often heard her mother say, "Get away from me! You stink!" Simply beginning to be aware of the messages keeps those messages from becoming triggers that lead us back to the addiction.

Sometimes in early recovery women are told to counter the negative voices and messages in their heads with "affirmations." I smile when I remember Nancy's response to that suggestion. She said, "Here's my affirmation. I look in the mirror and say 'You're a piece of scum. Just like my mom said.'" So we had to come up with another way of countering old negative thoughts.

What can you say or do when you are aware of a hurtful voice? One woman said, "I tell myself I don't ever have to feel that way about myself again. I am able to respond to this voice in a different way. I am response-able." She could listen to the old messages and feel helpless, or she could choose a new message. This is where we start. This self-awareness emerges as we *name* the issues that trip us up related to our self-image and self-esteem. There is an opening, a crack in the darkness. A tiny light shines into the emptiness. Once we better understand those voices and messages in our heads we can begin to choose our responses.

Old Rules

Nancy, as we have learned, grew up in an alcoholic and abusive home where she learned the three commandments known to all who share that sort of childhood: "Don't talk, don't feel, don't trust." We will talk about the impact of these rules in several chapters. For Nancy they saturated every part of her addiction. When she came into treatment, she didn't talk, and her body language told me she thought the sessions were fruitless and unproductive. Her eyes rarely met mine. Her shoulders rolled inward. When I asked Nancy open-ended questions such as "Tell me about…" she would imperceptibly shake her head and study her hands. After several counseling sessions of almost total silence, I remembered that she had once mentioned that she enjoyed drawing. I suggested that she bring in some of her paintings and charcoal sketches. Who would have thought that this diminutive plumber by trade was an artist by soul? She had never showed anyone her work. Not even her children, her sister, her parents, or her husband. By some act of grace, she began to trust our relationship enough to show some of them to me. This was how Nancy started her work of recovery.

You may be thinking that's all well and good for Nancy, but you don't draw or paint. The bigger point of healing for Nancy was not the art, but the fact that she made a choice she might not have even been aware of. She chose to trust. A trusting and safe relationship is essential to the work of recovery. Sometimes, however, finding such a relationship presents a challenge. How are we to risk finding a trusting relationship when often relationships in the past have not been safe? How do we find the courage to even look when we don't feel we are worth anyone else's investment? Remember how we are framing this discussion. *We heal and grow in relationship.* It is the place we begin to find our truth. Also be clear that, in a truly healing relationship, one person does not have power over the other person. In a healing relationship there is dependability, respect, care and understanding, listening, a sense of security. Go slowly and begin to dare to risk—this time not for the addiction but for your recovery.

TRANSFORM

Doing something other than staying in the addiction can be both liberating and frightening. It means we will be going deeper and deeper into our self-awareness. It means we will be using that self-awareness to make different decisions to create a new self-image. It means we must now face the denial we have used, the vulnerabilities from the past, and our present relationships. Decisions based on a new awareness of ourselves and a new sense of responsibility can be daunting. New decisions can change the relationships on which we base our self-image. New decisions mean we have to learn to trust but, if not in ourselves, then in whom? New decisions mean we might have to start to actually like ourselves. In practical terms it also means we must identify short-term achievable goals.

New Decisions and Small Successes

So often in addiction we feel we have no choice. The booze, the drugs, the rituals all feel so compulsive and automatic. At some level, however, we know that we can choose to change our connections with people, places, and things that set off the addictive ritual. Remember the tiger that creeps along in the tall grass next to you and, when you least expect it, jumps out and bites? Remember the voices, the messages?

"I'll just have two tonight. I can handle it."
"One will relax me."
"I'll just go to the bar to see my friends. Where's the harm in that?"
"He likes me to have a drink with him."

Any of those sound familiar?

It's at this point, when you begin to recognize the choices you have, you must notice also what your body is telling you. Do you hear the denial, the minimization, the rationalization, the justification? Do you feel the messages anywhere in your body? Do the voices create a tension, an anxiety?

One of my recovering friends describes her own thought process as a fierce struggle. After all the work of the day is done, she visualizes herself kicking back and sipping a big glass of whiskey or maybe smoking a joint. She tries to justify it in her mind by saying that she just wants some relief from the stress of the day, something that will take the edge off things. The only problem is that she knows if she drinks the whiskey or smokes the joint she will eventually lose everything she values in life. So she decides not to use today. Who knows about tomorrow but not now—not today. And if you crave the cocaine to be part of the crowd and the "fun," pass it up at least for tonight. This change in thought process and decision does not come early or easily, but it does come with each new decision and small successes.

Think about what you can do differently. Change the message in your head. Think through the drink or drug. What would you lose? On the other hand what would you gain? These can be difficult and painful decisions and choices. Ask yourself:

> *"What if I stopped seeing that particular person?"*
> *"What if I decided not to go to that particular place?"*
> *"What do I do when that certain person seems the one on whom I base my entire self-image and self-esteem?"*
> *"What if that place is where I feel I must go to have fun?"*

And then think again, how will it feel tomorrow when you know you made healthier choices, when you know you took care of your recovery? How will it feel to have a clear head no longer filled with guilt and remorse? What healing might come in the relationships you hold most dear?

What do you need to stay out of the denial, the minimization? Whom else can you be with? Whom can you trust? Remember the bad times. That's not to say you must wallow in the guilt and shame, but it is terribly important to remember the incidents, the DUIs, the confrontations at work, the embarrassments. *It really was bad!* You wouldn't be reading this book if it wasn't. And if it weren't truly that bad, I wouldn't be writing this! But remember, neither you nor I ever have to feel that way about ourselves again.

You begin to smile with each of your small successes. You can make recovery decisions. You can decide to treat yourself to a latte instead of a beer, to sit down and rest with a new magazine and a soda. You can go to a movie instead of the bar or suggest places other than a bar to meet your friend. You can change your phone number. With these small choices, you will begin to get brief glimpses of how your life could be different.

When you awaken in the morning, is there a different sense of what the day may bring? Is there hope? Are your eyes a little clearer? Does your skin begin to have some color? Are you sleeping better? Do you feel more alive? It's OK to notice that you feel brighter/prettier/happier! You will likely hear someone say, "It's nice to see you smile." Does it feel good to know you are building up some recovery time? Does the darkness begin to have more light?

Trust Your Healing Connections

As you begin to have recovery successes, you begin to trust yourself and others. You may find others who are struggling with similar demons, and they may be a bit further along than you are. Perhaps you'll find a self-help group, a church group, or a friend. Have a phone number handy (on your speed dial because in a crisis you can't waste time looking) of someone you trust enough to call when the going gets really tough. And it will. Or maybe you need to get rid of the cell phone completely if it's your line to your dealer!

Find something to read: a magazine, a mystery, a prayer book. Reading and meditation will interrupt your thoughts of using. Have a meditation book in your purse or in your drawer at work. (You'll find the names of some of my favorites at the back of this book.) Reread Psalm 91 about God saving us from "the terror of the night." It really is true, you can't think two thoughts at the same time. If you are focusing on recovery, you won't be concentrating on using.

Alcoholics Anonymous and sponsorship are very effective for some people. Meetings and sponsorship give you someone who has gone through what you are going through and knows what a craving is. A sponsor should be a woman—a woman whom you trust, a woman whom you respect and who respects you. A temporary sponsor gives you an opportunity to have a support person while you are meeting other women in the program. Some cities have meeting centers that are open all day and evening. These are safe places with other recovering people to talk with.

A therapist or counselor might be helpful too. A counselor helps you identify the short-term achievable goals, helps you with the tasks of recovery, and helps you sort through some of these issues and vulnerable spots. Sometimes women in recovery find it easier to trust a woman counselor. However, some of the most caring, effective counselors I know are men. It really is about the trusting relationship you establish with the counselor. If you feel safe and cared for, the trust can build and the work of recovery can be done.

In addition to an individual sponsor or therapist, you might consider involvement in a women's counseling group. It might be based on recovery or even the general issues every woman deals with. This type of group has healing features based on a woman's need to heal in relationship. These healing features in a women's group include a way to begin to understand we are not alone in our experience, to acknowledge that all the group participants have a connection, and to develop compassion for yourself and an openness and respect of others.

RELAPSE

You may find yourself wondering, what if relapse happens? Relapse is a part of this disease. Sometimes relapse is called a slip. I'm not sure that is an accurate term. If I slip on the sidewalk, it's generally because I didn't see a piece of ice or something else slippery. If I relapse, I really can see it coming. If I haven't paid attention to the triggers that set me up, it may feel like an unpredictable slipping; but when I deny and minimize the impact of the disease, when I stop paying attention to the people, places, and things that reignite the compulsion, I'm poised to slip. Someone once said a slip can be defined as *Sobriety Lost Its Priority*. It's an apt definition, for when we relapse or slip, something or someone else seemed more important. Sobriety lost its priority for us.

One of the big problems with relapse is that far too many people just give up after the first or fifth or twentieth relapse. The old voices of defeat and self-disgust take over. But addiction is a progressive, fatal disease. If you don't come back to active recovery, *you* will *die*...physically, emotionally, and spiritually. Each relapse teaches us something if we are willing to learn. What got in the way? What seemed more important? What did I lose this time?

As we talked about earlier, one of the things lost in relapse is the trust in self, trust in whether I can do this. After a relapse, often women return to treatment or counseling or self-help broken and chagrined. They've lost trust in themselves and are at risk of losing hope. The recovering community needs to hold them and hold onto them as the recovery continues.

A few years ago a woman of some renown was found unconscious on her front sidewalk. Her struggle with alcoholism had been public knowledge for many years. The innuendo in the press was that this was "yet another relapse." I was truly saddened by the news and thought about the public humiliation and personal desperation she might feel. Few of us have to endure such public humiliation. A friend and I were talking about it, and she said, "And you know she could have the best treatment available anywhere. Isn't anyone helping her?" I would guess she has help. But something is still missing.

The wife of a dentist friend is in treatment at one of the most prestigious centers money can buy, for the third time. She has had *years* of recovery. What happened? What is it we are missing? I pray someone is holding her and telling her she is loved. She must not lose hope.

Both the woman found on the sidewalk and the wife of the dentist may not yet understand how their self-image, their relationships, and their spiritual recovery are connected.

Reshaping Relationships

As the Stone Center says, we, as women, define ourselves and our self-image by how we take care of relationships. So we will talk about relationships with this issue of self-image, and we will also talk about relationships in each chapter. In recovery, especially fairly early, our personal relationships are cracking. The addiction was the priority, and this usually had a devastating impact on those we love. This devastating impact is often what motivates us to take those initial steps into recovery. Fractured relationships may take a long time to repair. In the meantime we need connection with those who understand the struggle and are willing to be in relationship with us.

Marriage and Relationships

If we agree with the Stone Center that being in a caring relationship is essential to a woman's positive self-image, it's important to consider how self-image connects with the many, varied relationships in our recovery journey. One critically important relationship is that of partner/wife/spouse. The marital relationship usually takes a heavy blow during our addiction. In treatment programs in the not-too-distant past counselors advised, "Don't worry about the marriage. If you stop drinking, the marriage will stabilize itself." The general feeling was that the first year of recovery had to be focused only on stopping the addiction—the drinking or the drugging.

Unfortunately, all too often the marriage doesn't survive the first year of recovery! Think about what has happened. The addiction was her number one priority. She became isolated. Every time she spoke, she sounded bitter and angry. She spent money they didn't have. Her husband or partner had to call in sick for her. Numerous times. He had to prepare meals. He had to lie. To their children he may have had to say, "Mom's not feeling good." And now that she's in a recovery program, he's hopeful. But he wants it fixed all at once. Sometimes he doesn't seem to have a clue about the struggle. He'll push. All too often a conversation goes something like this:

> Husband: "So what should I do when you start to have that attitude again?"
> She: "What attitude? What about your attitude?"
> The fight explodes, and the tiger jumps out of the grass.
> She (to herself): "A joint/a snort/a shot/a pill would calm me down."

Neither partner learns how to be gentle right away. Nor do we learn how to be honest overnight. After listening to many stories, I have come to believe that as the feelings of guilt about drinking/drugging begin to subside, there is a much better chance that the recovering woman can more clearly explore and acknowledge the issues. She then may be able to say, "Tell me how you know when my attitude is changing. What do I say? What do I sound like?"

Trust begins to grow. Intimacy unfolds. Sometimes this new communication is best and most safely accomplished with a counselor. Inpatient and outpatient treatment programs often have family night meetings. These can be both educational and therapeutic. But what happens when treatment is over? It is very important to recognize this powerful relationship component of recovery and consider ongoing couples' therapy.

Parenting Relationships

Another vital relationship in our recovery in this stage of *transforming* our self-image is our relationship with our children. Recovery relationships with children have many layers. As parents we must ask, "What happened to my parenting skills during the addiction? Did I ever have good parenting skills?" Most of us parent the way we were parented. It's sort of like cooking. Unless we go to cooking school, or thumb through cooking magazines, most of us cook the way our mothers cooked. On the other hand, maybe we parent exactly the *opposite* of the way we were parented because we swear we'll *never* be like our parents. We need to look at what's worked and what hasn't. What are our children doing well in? How can we support that? Are we thrusting them into caretaking roles for which they are ill prepared? Are they angry, hurt, lost? How do we know?

Several months after my husband's military move and my failed geographic "cure" I finally "named the problem." I started attending self-help. Since going to self-help meant being away from home several evenings a week, I decided I needed to tell my children where I was going those nights. After all, I didn't want them to think I was going to a bar! I had been a closet drinker, not one to go to bars. Some weeks later my eleven-year-old daughter complained that I was not there to settle her into bed and say prayers at night. I admitted to myself that "settling her into bed" really had meant an excuse to pass out in her bed. I reaffirmed to her that I had been drinking too much and needed help. I asked how we could have that special time in another way. So we came up with a new plan; we said prayers before I left for meetings and started having lunch on Saturdays—just the two of us with time to talk and shop and have fun.

A few months into my initial foray into recovery this same

daughter asked from the back seat of the car, "So, Mom, when did you decide you were an alcoholic?" The daughter had just named it—nailed it—no holds barred! *I* might have had trouble naming it, but she certainly didn't! Later this precious child said, "Mom, you're so much nicer since you've stopped drinking." These were heart-wrenching important messages about my drinking and my relationship with her. I needed to hear them physically, emotionally, and spiritually.

There are many other parental relationship issues besides honesty and trust issues that affect our self-esteem and self-image as mothers. We need to set boundaries, help with homework, supervise chores—all the things children of alcoholics and addicts have had only sporadically. And we must admit that it is we who are responsible for that lack of consistency. How do we fix it? Very slowly. We get help. We read books. We go for counseling. We take a couple of parenting classes. We talk with the teachers. We seek support and resources from the school counselor. We reinforce the positive behavior and ignore the negative. We ask these wounded children how they are feeling. We listen! With no other distractions. We hold them, and we tell them they are the most important part of our lives. We cherish and treasure them.

Discovering Gifts

Women approach their recoveries each in their own unique ways. For instance, Nancy worked to *transform* her self-image by drawing and painting. And she dared to share the drawings and paintings. She stayed in individual counseling. No groups for this girl. And when we met, she had pictures tucked under her arm. The first picture she showed me was one she called *The Silent Scream*. It is reminiscent of the famous late–nineteenth-century Norwegian painting by Edvard Munch, but this one was all hers. She explained why the colors were all black. She talked about the rage she had inside. She talked about the grief she had never shared. Over the next months and years the colors of Nancy's pictures became lighter. The images moved from rage and anger to pastoral scenes—scenes she thought I might enjoy. And she shared a slight smile when I would genuinely admire her work. She began to reach out. She spent more time with her granddaughter. She went canoeing. "I haven't done that in years," she said.

She risked. She stumbled. She returned. One significant step on her path to recovery happened when she attended a painting workshop put on by a religious retreat house for a weekend. It wasn't a perfect recovery episode but a recovery step. She had done well the first day of the workshop, but trouble reared its head on the second day when they were to paint in a cemetery. Her son, David, had committed suicide only a few years earlier, and she had used her addiction to bury her grief and sadness. For the first time in recovery she faced the reality of his death, and she wasn't prepared for that powerful trigger. So she went out and bought a case of beer and drank it because that's what had worked in the past.

That evening I received a call from the minister of the retreat house. He told me about the episode and asked me to be gentle with her. He said Nancy expected me to yell at her because yelling was what she had always experienced when she screwed up before. He put Nancy on and I listened to her as she told me what happened at the workshop, and I told her I loved her and would see her Monday when she returned. Confrontation was the last thing Nancy needed just then. When she returned on Monday she didn't need to analyze the whole experience. She just needed to experience the grief. She needed to tell me about her son's death, about what had happened and what she felt. She needed to tell me the story. And she needed me to hold her literally and figuratively. Sometime later she would begin to consider what David's death had done to her sense of self and how she might think about that differently.

As she left my office that day she even managed a grin and said, "Well, at least I didn't go for the cocaine." That's recovery!

So at this early stage we begin to make new decisions and acknowledge the small successes. We pay attention to the messages and voices in our heads. We identify short-term goals and concrete ways to attain them. We make new connections; we acknowledge the potential for relapse; we examine relationships; we discover gifts. We celebrate the successes, and we examine our further challenges. Like Nancy, we can begin to smile a crooked smile knowing that we can turn the biblical quotation around and begin to love ourselves as we love our neighbor.

SUSTAIN

Though *sustain* is presented in this book as the "third" stage of recovery, please know that this exploration of the spiritual core of our recovery is there from the very beginning. It is there when we *name* the issues. It is there when we *transform* some thinking and behaviors. And it is surely there as we *sustain* this recovery at our spiritual core.

We might call this new awareness of the spiritual core of recovery developing a new awareness of our relationship with God. This relationship *sustains* us through the tough times. We'll talk about it again and again as we contemplate other recovery topics in further chapters.

What gives us the strength to keep going when the pain and struggle seem impossible? When our relationships are full of anger, when the trust in ourselves and others feels empty, when our self-esteem is battered and we feel no joy, where do we turn? We begin with an openness to an exploration of our relationship with a divine presence, with God.

A Relationship With God

How do we begin? We start with the same openness we have been talking about. We listen to the messages inside, we find people we can trust, and we risk. Nancy grew up thinking God was somebody to stay away from. Her mother warned her, "God will get you for that!" She also learned God loved other people, "just not me."

Where did *you* learn about God? What were the messages? Was God loving or punishing? Was God "going to get you for that"? Or was God filled with love and forgiveness?

BROKEN

Nancy continued, "Once there was a contest on a cereal box. To win the contest you had to name a horse. The prize was a stay at Roy Rogers' ranch. I wanted to win that contest in the worst way!" Nancy told this story with a yearning still for that place where she could be safe. A ranch. Away from the abuse that permeated her home. But she also knew she would not win. "God loved other people, but not me. I wasn't lovable. I was something that just had to be here. When I was eight or nine years old my mother said, 'I wish I would have flushed you down the toilet when I had a chance.' She told me other people didn't like me. I was fat, and lazy and ugly. When we were teenagers she would buy my sister clothes at the department store but bought my clothes at the dollar store. When I asked her why she did that she said, 'You're going to look like s**t anyway.'"

Nancy started praying again when she had her first baby. "I know you don't love me but you love this baby. Help David-baby." Nancy said that when she got away from her parents and had her baby she began to realize, "God did love me. He gave me this beautiful baby....Now I know it." When I asked her to think about how she began to know it, she talked of a picture that was next to her bed as a child. Maybe you know the picture. It is of a guardian angel with her wing protectively sheltering two children as they cross a bridge in a storm. Nancy asked God to protect this baby as she had wanted that guardian angel to protect her. It was a prayer—maybe not for herself yet, but a tap on the door.

Nancy also spoke (and still speaks) lovingly of the pastor/counselor, Joe, who helped her gain recovery through her relationship with God. She said she was able to picture God through him. She used words to describe this pastor/counselor as "gentle, loving, compassionate, protector, healer...accepting, unconditional." He helped her face it and embrace it—no matter what "it" was. He was with her through the brokenness, through the shame.

Nancy hears Joe's message about recovery. Joe's message is the belief that it is a need to move out of this shame that compels us to set long-term recovery in the context of an ongoing relationship with God. Sustained, joyous recovery is found only by knowing and believing we belong to and are loved by God. This is the real miracle of recovery. A woman addict or alcoholic or shoplifter or sexual addict belongs to and is loved by God, *no matter what.* Our addiction can make us lose everything: job, kids, husband, house, even our belief in who we are. We are left with only shame. But when we begin to believe we are loved and we belong to God, unconditionally, we can begin to be open to a new message and a new life.

Joe continues to talk with Nancy and has some wonderful things to say about this kind of new relationship—a relationship with God based on goodness and grace. He constantly emphasizes God's promise of grace. He says that God's love for us is not dependent on our behavior but rather his acceptance of us is rooted and grounded in his love for us. God claims us not because of our behavior but because of who he is. He is like the father in the parable of the Prodigal Son who yearns for us to come home. When he sees us coming up the road he throws open the door of his house and embraces us and welcomes us home.

At the end of this book you'll find Joe's retelling of the biblical story of the Prodigal Son in "daughter" language. It might mirror your own struggle with demons and how you find your way back home. It's the story of what happens when the daughter goes off to the "far country" and squanders all her inheritance money. She buys wine, booze, pills, cocaine, crack, sex. The kids are left with neighbors in the city and finally they are taken by social services. They've been in foster home after foster home since then. The money is gone, and she's sleeping in the stairwell. Maybe she was just released from jail. She picks the garbage cans for food.

Or maybe the "prodigal daughter" is a respectable accountant or a nurse and the inheritance she squanders is the trust others have placed in her. She steals money to buy cocaine. She steals a patient's pain pills to cure her migraine. She goes to work drunk. Finally in desperation one night she cries out, "My God, what am I going to do about this?" She remembers something about God's love. Something she learned in Sunday school or something from prayers at night. "Jesus loves me, this I know...." There is hope. Hope that God will make it right. All she has to do is turn toward home. She can let go of all of her efforts to do it right, to rectify the past, to eradicate the shame. God/Mother is there, watching for her, waiting with her arms open wide, and runs out to meet her. She will kill the fatted calf. She will throw a huge barbecue as only Mama can. God has already forgiven, accepted, and restored her. Joe's epilogue is a powerful summary of the relationship with God we are talking about all through this book.

Besides scriptural stories and parables current spiritual writers also help us know of God's unconditional love. One writer who talks of our struggles being held within a relationship with God is Henri Nouwen. In his book *Life of the Beloved* (see References) Nouwen's discussion of the journey into that relationship is accepting that we are both broken and blessed. (Given the title of this book, it is clear Nouwen's writing had an impact on my recovery.) Understanding this idea of moving from broken to blessed in a relationship with God is crucial to our *sustained* recovery. In recovery we bring that wisdom into everything we say and do. Nancy knew well the "broken" part. Eventually she learned the blessed...and brought it into everything she says and does.

BLESSED

Is there someone or someplace in your life, like Nancy's pastor, who begins to help you feel safe? Who provides you a few minutes or hours at Roy Rogers' ranch? Who begins to give you a sense there can be a relationship with God? Could it simply be the stillness, the quiet prayer?

In the beginning of this chapter we talked about the power of the relationship with our parents. We said, particularly for a woman, the relationship with her mother frames who she comes to believe she is. It might have been a supportive, nurturing relationship. It is the one that "counts." More often than not, unfortunately, women in recovery remember the pain and hurt of the relationship with their mothers. This is not to say mothers are responsible for our addiction. *We* are responsible for our addiction, and we are response-able for our recovery. In the process of growing up and in the process of addiction, our fragile self-image was battered, bruised, and nearly destroyed by old messages, chaotic circumstances, and our own behaviors. Scriptural reading, spiritual authors, prayer, and other people who value what God is doing in their lives can help us reach the point Nancy finally grasped. *I* am chosen and loved by God. God yearns to have a relationship with *me!* It isn't something *I* have to do. It's not another task of recovery. If I'm open to God, I'll begin to understand what a loving parent really means—one who longs to give me gifts of peace, gentleness, power, and purpose, who takes me into this new relationship.

Somewhere, deep in our core, we can say yes to this inner truth that we are beloved daughters of God, and it changes everything. At every point from now on we have the choice to say yes or no. Each one of us yearns for peace, gentleness, and joy in our lives. Very often, we find that peace and joy through our suffering, as strange as that may sound. Through this suffering we are presented with the possibility of putting our addiction to death. However, if we choose our addiction, it means we are closing ourselves off from God's love. But God doesn't give up on us. God yearns be in a relationship with us. Even when we screw up. Even when we take the drink or the drug again, God continues to say, "Come home again; I love you no matter what. All is forgiven." This is God's promise. Our broken selves continue to be blessed.

This is the core truth. *You are loved.* You hear this truth from your own center. Each time you breathe, hear the voice that calls you *"My daughter."* The whole universe, earth, moon, and stars say, "Yes!" to you. And yes to your brokenness.

Things to *Think About*

1. What kind of impact did your addiction have on your self-image?
2. How will you think of yourself differently if you stop using?
3. At this point in your life, how do you think of your relationship with God?

CHAPTER • 2

T: Traditional roles

*M*y mother was a traditional, stay-at-home mom. She kept the house immaculate, complained about the mud we tracked in, smiled little, and criticized much. Mostly she criticized my dad's drinking...and all the problems that came from that drinking. My early recollections of her are dark, sad, and angry. Even a generation later my niece remembers being "afraid" of her during visits. When Dad would leave on binges Mom would worry out loud, "What will I do if he doesn't come back? How will I support you kids?" Her fear of my dad's drinking and his loss of jobs left her incredibly insecure. Mom's anxiety told me I needed a career in which I had job security and, more important, financial security. Her lack of confidence greatly influenced my choice to be a nurse. "You can always get a job as a nurse" or "You can marry a doctor" were messages I frequently heard. Later she softened and came to some peace. But those early messages had a profound impact on the traditional roles I chose, the way I assumed the responsibilities within those roles, and the relationships I formed along the way.

Think of all the roles you play: wife, mother, significant other, friend, cook, laundress, chauffeur, employee, cheerleader, gardener, computer technician, volunteer, secretary, student, scheduler, shopper, daughter, sister, artist, and probably many others. Most of these roles can be filled by either men or women; however, the roles are unique when considered from a woman's perspective. Traditional roles, with their gender-specific responsibilities and relationships, are influenced by many dynamics: the families we grew up in, our culture and its messages, the religious doctrines we heard. The roles themselves influence our addictions and recovery.

This chapter builds and expands on concepts discussed in Chapter 1. In the *name* section of Chapter 1 we explored how significant people and culture determine the way we think about ourselves and about our personal value. In this chapter of Traditional Roles, we examine how people and culture define the roles we choose, the responsibilities we assume within the roles, and the relationships we develop while fulfilling the roles. In the first stage of recovery *(name)* in traditional roles we consider how those roles ultimately influence addiction and recovery. First we consider what is "normal" development for girls and women. Normal healthy development, in a gender-specific model, involves the establishment of relationships in which there is mutual give-and-take, where each person works to understand what the other person is experiencing. These relationships, ones in which power and responsibility are shared, are discussed in this chapter as *the* primary roles for women. We also examine the roles of the specific family we grew up in and the culture and religions in which we were raised. We consider how women's roles enlarge or diminish us and how they influence our addiction and ultimately our recovery.

The second stage of *transform* acknowledges what needs to be shaped or reshaped in our roles for the changes into this new life of recovery. The role of "addict" creates a fear deep in our core. The change necessary to diminish that fear requires energy and courage. This energy comes from the healthy relationships we establish as we move into recovery. The energy we gain from these healthy relationships is our power. Use of our power gives us the courage to *transform* old patterns. It's time to explore questions

that challenge the social roles we choose and to explore new options and relationships that support recovery.

And in the *sustain* stage of recovery we examine the slow
spiritual process of healing that strengthens our roles in recovery.
We explore the *sanctity* of our roles, daily tasks, responsibilities,
relationships, and long-term choices. We strengthen our recovery
by finding inner quiet, a gentleness. It is there we find the sacredness of our roles within our relationship with God. What is this
new thing going on in our lives? Do we know we are blessed and
beloved? How can we be in that space more fully? Are we aware
of this emerging relationship with God?

NAME

What is "normal" healthy development for women? Decades ago,
psychological theories equated healthy development for both boys
and girls in models of being strongly independent individuals, of
being separate from one another. Normal development for everyone
meant "being your own man," standing up for yourself, making it
on your own. More recently, gender-specific developmental theories such as those of the Stone Center acknowledge that childhood
expectations and normal development for girls are different from
what normal development is for boys. Both are valid, just different.

That said, there are many examples where these cultural expectations and gender-specific examples are not the norm. Many
families work very hard to expose both boys and girls to many
different experiences and let the child determine where his or her
strengths and interests lie in the roles the child chooses. Also today
many children are raised in single-parent families where roles are
learned from a variety of adults. As mentioned in the Introduction
and Chapter 1, in this discussion we are using the research from
the Stone Center that specifically explores the impact of families

and culture on the development of girls and women. This research indicates that though there are many individual differences in raising girls, there remain many gender-specific cultural expectations for women today.

All too often the expectation from families and society remains that women fulfill all those roles we listed above and fulfill them "perfectly"—a complex and, at times, monumental activity. However, it is an activity for which we, as women, have been trained and trained well. The training for us to fulfill multiple roles perfectly has been part of our development and our education.

As with the development of our self-image, even today the traditional role training begins at home. Generally, dads are off to work and boys go out to play. Boys are encouraged to develop independence and self-mastery. As we said earlier, independence and self-mastery were long believed to be hallmarks of normal development for all children—boys and girls. But boys play competitive games and learn to be warriors: cowboys and Indians, Dungeons and Dragons, Capture the Flag, and videogames. They learn their roles in social experiences out of the house with buddies or competing in action videos of aggressiveness, violence, and killing. Often, they learn these roles from Dad. The goal is to win and not be a loser.

In contrast, little girls stay close to mother and learn women's multiple roles. If they don't have a mother, there is usually another woman who is their role model. Of course today many mothers go to work also, but when they are home they still perform most of the traditional roles. Social research indicates that, even when working full-time out of the home, women continue to provide most of the cooking, cleaning, and child-care tasks. Girls learn "good" mothering (based on gentleness and meeting a child's needs) or "bad" mothering (based on stress, anxiety, and fear). Little girls carefully observe how mother responds to people, places, and

things. Little girls play games of "house" and school and Barbie...
all about themselves in relation to others.

The Primary Role of Women: Building and Maintaining Relationships

Although women fulfill multiple roles, theories of healthy women's
development indicate that *the* primary role of women is to establish
give-and-take, to foster mutual relationships. The healthy woman
learns to be connected with another person in a way that respects
and cares about the other person. And when she is in a healthy
relationship the other person respects and cares for her on an equal
basis. In healthy relationships based on shared connections, one
person does not hold power over the other. Honorable connections show women who they are at their core. Being responsible
for others and caring for others is a good thing! It is not the *goal*
of women to establish healthy relationships. But rather, women's
primary role is to establish these relationships. It is what we do
and who we are—and we are very good at it! Mutual relationships
hold us and embrace us as we heal and grow.

Being in Relation

In healthy families a girl learns to be responsible and caring by
paying attention to how her mother is feeling and acting. How
does mother respond to a particular situation? What is mother
saying? What is she doing? Do her words and actions fit together?
For this capacity of mutual connectedness to develop, there also
needs to be a mutual sharing process between mother and daughter.
Through this relationship, the daughter develops self-esteem and
a sense of knowing how to understand and respond to the needs
and feelings of others.

As the mother-daughter relationship grows over the life cycle, a
young woman develops her own method of being in a relationship.

It becomes her style. During adolescence this mother-daughter relationship can be particularly complex as the daughter's sense of self changes. Very often, the daughter begins to feel the need to put off or even ignore her own priorities (such as the relationship with her mother) to be "in relationship" with other significant peers—especially boys. It can be a time of yelling and slamming doors. Dated psychological theories argue that adolescent girls' need to be independent is the cause of the estrangement between mother and daughter. In newer women's development theory, the adolescent girl is not seen as needing to separate from mother but rather wanting to change the type of this relationship. This desire develops as other relationships in her life are beginning to take priority. But even this conflict with mother can be a form of connection, a way of learning to be in relation. Young women who have mothers with a strong sense of their own "self" can begin to learn to work out differences in relationships without disconnecting from the person they care about (mother).

Role Development

In addition to mother and home, culture and society also have a strong impact on young women. School, play, church, and the media greatly affect our role development. Just as with parents, the influence can range from very positive to devastating.

For example, Nancy remembers little about school. The person Nancy remembers as most caring was the school nurse. "She always 'saved' me. She brought me new clothes. The ones I had were so ugly and shameful—sometimes just a slip. In fourth grade, she saved me when I turned in a paper that didn't follow instructions. The teacher laughed at me, and I threw a book at her and then began beating her up. The nurse took me to her office, and I never had to go back to that teacher's class again. I wanted to be a nurse, but I got married at sixteen. My mother wanted me out of the house so she gave permission. She blamed me after my father left. He had raped me for years. He finally left, and my mother said it was my fault. And then later the person I looked up to most was my husband's mother—Ma. Her husband had been an alcoholic but she stayed. She raised nine kids. She was a saint."

Girls watch and learn.

School has a strong impact on women's lifelong roles as learners and teachers. Feedback from teachers, report cards, and especially peers' comments have a connection between self-image and the traditional roles we were assigned or chose. "The brain, teacher's pet, brownnose, dork, stupid, A student, D student" were titles that told us who we were and what role in the classroom, crowd, or family we would play. They told us whether we were responsible persons or failures. Either we worked hard to maintain that role or we became discouraged and gave up.

Another area of society where girls begin to assume roles and relationships very differently from boys is in play and group activities. For boys, the rules of the game and winning are important. For girls, the priority is to be in relationships with the other participants. When playing a team game or in a group activity, girls focus on how the players relate to each other—not just the rules and the right way to play or accomplish the task. In group activities such as bands, theater, and clubs girls learn how to plan, work together, and get things done.

Friends, peer groups, social circles, and advertising tell young girls who they are. The teen crowd decides who is "popular, wild, cute" or "wallflower, strange, weird." Advertising preaches that thin is the only sexy size. Currently there is a girls' teen T-shirt imprinted across the breast area: "If you have these, who needs brains!"

Girls watch and learn.

Certainly women's sports activities have created increased opportunities for development of different relationships and roles over the last few decades. Beyond the technical skills learned, the relationships, the cohesiveness, the team dynamics provide energy. These opportunities have expanded leadership roles, assertiveness techniques, and reciprocal relationships. A young friend who struggles with eating issues played girls' softball in high school and talks with great fondness of the laughter and relationships of those times. She rarely mentions a play or a score or a particular game. She continues to have many friends, and she places a very high priority on her relationships. She runs marathons but always runs with a girlfriend. They train and work out on weekends and play along with the achievement. "I wouldn't be doing this if Karen wasn't running it with me." She and Karen ran a recent marathon and stayed together the whole distance regardless of the time clock. "I told her I'd run it with her. I told her I'd stay with her. I don't care how fast I ran it."

Her husband ran the same marathon. "I'm doing this as an experiment. I've prepared more thoroughly this time with workouts and diet. I'll snack more frequently and drink a lot more fluid." After the marathon he commented, "My time was 4:15. Did you see the wheels came off in the final three miles? I did OK for the time I trained."

Neither is right or wrong...just different.

Another place many of us learned about roles and relationships was in church. Some of us attended a church-run school with uniforms, codes, and rituals. Maybe we attended Sunday school with lessons, beliefs, doctrines. Or we listened to scripture and sermons that told us about our roles and responsibilities as women. The message I clearly heard was, "Be perfect....Be saintly....If you are naughty, God will be angry." Did a particular church teach you about women's roles, responsibilities, and relationships? What do you remember learning from them? Are those messages you still hear in your head?

In summary, in "normal" healthy development we, as women, are greatly influenced by our mothers. Social networks and society also impact our development, but they are secondary to the influence of mother. In healthy development the primary role of women is to establish relationships in which each person cares for the other and works to understand the experience of the other. In developing these relationships, women take on roles and responsibilities that make us feel we are in relationship with the other person.

But what if our development was not normal and healthy ? What if we didn't learn to seek strong give-and-take relationships? What if performing the roles we are in challenges our recovery?

Role Development
Within the Disease of Addiction

Given that we are women with issues of addiction and given that addiction has a strong family and genetic component, there is a very good chance that many of us grew up in situations that would not be considered normal. In families where addiction is present, or families with secrets, or families with violence, or many kinds of other struggles, assigned roles and unspoken rules develop that allow the family to appear normal to the outside world. But these assigned roles and unspoken rules are confusing and frightening. Children in families struggling with addiction are often assigned a particular role or learn to follow an unspoken rule. The tragedy is that the child often remains stuck there.

Though the roles and rules in a family with addiction are generally presented in substance abuse literature as restrictive and negative, it is important to acknowledge that these rules and roles also perform a stabilizing function. Let's remember that these family members are struggling with the potentially fatal disease of a loved one. They are in recurring crisis. They are functioning in what seems to them the only way to avoid a catastrophe. They are doing the very best they can. The roles and rules allow the family to seem to be in balance.

A family dealing with the behaviors and chaos of an addiction is similar to a mobile placed over a baby's crib. If anyone bumps a part of the mobile or removes a piece, the entire mobile loses balance and swings, sometimes becoming entangled, swinging out of control, or collapsing onto the floor. People in a family with addiction are assigned and assume the roles (various characters on the mobile) in an attempt to maintain the fragile balance in an unstable environment, and the addicted person's behavior is constantly taking a whack at the entire mobile. But as we move in recovery when the particular roles and rules of our childhoods are *named* and examined, there is an opportunity to discover whether we are stuck in them and whether they place our recovery at risk. This discovery can be creative, courageous, healthy, and exciting.

The Roles in a Family With Addiction

The material on roles in families with addictions was initially developed in the 1980s by various therapists including John Ackerman, Claudia Black, and John Bradwell. They identified patterns of behaviors in family members where addiction was a problem. These patterns of behaviors were individually named, and they became "roles in the family." The role names, the behaviors, and what they described became shorthand for helping families discover the dynamics of their situations:

- *Enabler:* Often associated with the spouse of the addict; his or her behavior (unwittingly) allows the disease to progress; "codependent" was a frequent label for this person
- *Hero:* The "perfect" child, often the firstborn, successful, mannerly—makes the family look good

- *Scapegoat:* Acts out the turmoil in the family; gets into trouble—lies/steals/fights—takes the focus off the addicted person
- *Lost child:* The quiet one who goes to her or his room; isolates
- *Mascot:* The jokester who makes everyone laugh and provides comic relief

Of course not every family with an addicted person has four children. A child can assume more than one role, or a specific role may be absent in a particular family. Essentially, the goal of these roles is to take the focus off the real problem—the person with the addiction—and keep the mobile very, very still so no one will know. And the disease progresses.

When these role names first came into use in the field of addiction, they helped conceptualize patterns and groups of behaviors seen in family members of persons with addiction. Unfortunately as the terms became more familiar, they evolved in popular psychology as diagnoses of any and all family members, even in families without addiction problems. The term "dysfunctional family" became so overused, it was hard to believe there were any "normal" families anywhere.

Another of the problems with overuse of labels is the implication that the person being labeled is part of the problem. We begin to believe that the "enabler" or the "hero" or any of the other roles causes at least part of the problem. The reality is that children who grow up in families where a parent has an addiction are incredibly courageous and strong. They have learned to survive sad and frightening circumstances by developing a certain way of relating, a role that works for them. It protects them and decreases their anxiety. But the tragic difficulty with this survival technique lies in the probability that these persons will limit the way they relate to the "real world." They will relate to everyone in their life by acting out "their role" because the behavior feels safe, protective.

But that role is much too restrictive. If a person is going to engage fully in life, love, work, and society, she needs a whole variety of ways to interact and relate with other people to be her authentic self. Identifying our place in these various roles is a valuable exercise. We begin to see patterns, responsibilities we take on, and causes of our anxieties.

The person who assumes the enabler role defined above was often also labeled as codependent. This was a useful term in early theory development to describe certain behaviors, but overuse has worn it out to the point of irrelevance. All of the roles in substance-abusing families came to be seen as leading to co-dependency. Co-dependency has many definitions, but generally it is described as a set of behaviors in which a person is painfully dependent on the approval of others. This approval feels like safety, identity, and self-worth. Co-dependent people were and still are often viewed as obsessed or preoccupied with controlling the behavior of the addicted person. Anyone from such a family is seen as needing to control all other people, places, and things. However, over the years, the term has been used by people who take on that label as a defense, an excuse, a justification. Some people even use the label as a reason to stop doing the nurturing, caring things that are part of a mature relationship. The label also stops the exploration of the feelings underneath their behavior. And some people have used the label as an apology for their own behavior. They neglect to explore what role they want instead, what responsibilities they have for their own lives, what choices they have to change their own circumstances. One woman was told in a group to stop fixing her husband's lunch for work because that was codependent. He worked on an asphalting crew in an isolated, rural area with no Subway or McDonald's nearby. He was an alcoholic. She was angry. The group was angry. Focusing on the label of codependent instead of what she was feeling stopped the discussion of what was underneath her feelings: her helplessness, her fear, her seeming lack of options. Labels cut off exploration of feelings. Currently in the field of addiction the concept of co-dependency is used with a strong sense of balance. There are people who have had significant hardships because they are in a committed relationship with an addict. But not every person in that kind of relationship is codependent.

The Unspoken Rules

In families with substance abuse issues, in addition to roles they used to survive, children were taught rules to keep the mobile from collapsing. We named these rules before, and they are core to the way we carry out our roles and relationships. These rules are

"Don't talk."
"Don't feel."
"Don't trust."

These rules are threaded through many of the challenges to recovery in the STIGMA model and will be referred to again in several chapters. They apply powerfully to traditional roles, responsibilities, and relationships. Accepting these rules as "rules to live by" keeps us isolated. We don't learn to communicate. We deny our feelings. We don't risk in relationship. The world is unsafe. We are afraid. We find that a drink, a drug, a cut relieves the stress, the fear, the anxiety.

"Don't talk."

That rule came across in our house in several different ways. "Stay out of his way....Shh....Don't upset him." Well into adulthood I did not want to "upset" anyone. Even in a time of profound grief, I did not share with those I loved. I didn't want to upset them.

"Don't feel."

In our house exploration of feelings was nonexistent. The feeling of anger simply was not allowed. I grew up with "Don't show it." As a result, anger has always frightened me. Tears, sadness, disappointment made me feel powerless and were tolerated only in quiet, controlled expressions. Even excitement or joy was to be muted and quiet. In retrospect neither of my parents had ever learned about feelings in their families. My parents were good people who loved my brother and me beyond measure. They simply did not know a different way of being in relationship, given the chaotic families from which they came. This multigenerational perspective is an important consideration. If addiction is a disease with a strong genetic component, it is useful to consider the families from which our parents came. Looking back through their parents and grandparents, it is sometimes staggering to see the thread of the disease.

"Don't trust."

Don't trust the addict....He always lets you down. Don't trust anyone outside the family....We have to look perfect. Don't trust your own feelings.... Minimize this—it isn't happening—it isn't that bad." With this rule we lose the ability to trust the family, to trust others, and to trust our own instincts, our own gut, and our own selves. Then in the progression of our own addiction we give further life to this rule. Eventually, we lose the ability to trust ourselves. After all, how many times have we promised ourselves we will never do that again: never drink that much...never spend that much on the drug...never leave the children for the night... never drive drunk again...never make that phone call...never do that drug deal? And how many times have we done it again? It happens over and over, and we lose any sense of trust in our own word. We see our role as the addicted failure. What happened to that "perfect" little girl? Where do we turn?

Where do you turn?

TRANSFORM

The adult roles and relationships in which we as women with addictions find ourselves are often determined by both the learning that takes place for girls in our culture and the rules and roles we saw played out in our family. Often these roles and relationships are restrictive, isolated, sad, and lonely disconnections. All too often stress and anxiety threaten our recovery and trigger our relapse. The role of "addict" creates its own incredible stress, anxiety and fear in the relationships we try to maintain. In this stage of *transform* we consider ways to reshape the roles, rules, and relationships. We explore new ways to mold our recovery. The background for our recovery in this stage is within healthy relationships. As we said in the Self-image section, healthy relationships provide power. Power gives us the energy and courage to take risks, try new ways of being, new ways of relating...to create, to change.

Strong Healthy Relationships

A basic sense of connection holds us and gives us a sense of power. It is not "power over," which our competitive society says is the goal. This power is the energy of everyday living, of being "in relation." It is the understanding we learned from a healthy mother. It is the energy we feel when we know we are capable of accomplishing what we want in everyday life. Mutual relationships make us genuine and accountable. They foster healing and honor our roles and responsibilities.

This healing power within relationships is what moves us in "becoming." It helps us to be more fully alive and competent.

These relationships inspire us to care about other people and other things in a very broad way. These relationships acknowledge that we affect the other person and that the person affects us. We are open to the impact these relationships have on us. Identifying and building relationships with these traits takes risk, courage, strength, and creativity. It may require change in your roles and relationships with certain people, places, and things.

Changing Roles and Fear

Change is both scary and exciting. Change requires action. Change can lead to conflict. Very few people like change, even change they see as positive. They especially dislike it if the change affects them. Some of your new choices, your new actions in recovery will lead to change and conflict in your roles and relationships. Conflict often feels like disconnection. It feels like we will lose the relationship. We fear our relationships will be destroyed. For the changes necessary to support recovery, it is important that we acknowledge our own fears and the fears of others affected by our changes. We begin to change the rules, the roles, and the relationships. We begin to talk, to feel, to trust.

For example, we break the rule of "don't talk." We risk telling the secret. We tell what is going on with us. We dare to share with someone we trust: "I'm not certain what's going on, but I'm scared. I think I'm drinking/using too much....I'm afraid I'll get caught. I'm afraid they'll find out....I think I'm losing control. I have to do something about this." We risk asking questions. "What do you think about this? What if I have to quit? How will you feel about that? What about us? What do you think I should do?"

We confront the rule of "don't feel." We no longer deny the feelings, fear, or excitement. "If I have to give it up I won't have any fun anymore. I might lose all my friends. But if I don't give it up what if I get arrested? What if I lose my kids?" These stressful feelings can create an endless cycle of relapse. If we get stuck in the fear, we use again. To make the change, we need to get a glimpse of how it will feel to lessen the fear...to feel anticipation that life might be different.

In this stage of *transform* it is important to move from the feeling of fear and begin to think about the joy and freedom that comes with losing the fear. What would it feel like never to have to be fearful about the addiction again? What would it feel like to know at your core you are living the life you want—responsible, loving, and blessed.

Changing Roles and Stress

When you listed the many roles, responsibilities, and relationships you fill on a daily basis, which were the ones you most enjoy? Which ones give you the most stress? Create the anxiety? Which were the ones that put you at risk of using again?

Let's take a minute to talk about stress. Stress certainly can be a trigger for relapse. To diminish stress we need to become more aware of our bodies and the signals it gives us when we are under stress: the headache, the tightened shoulders, the pinched mouth, the clenched jaw or fist. Are you aware of when your body is giving you a signal that you are under stress? Short-term stress management emphasizes the practice of identifying the area where you hold the stress, then tensing that area for about ten seconds, and then relaxing the area of the body in which you are holding the stress. Tighten your shoulders, hold them tight for about ten seconds, and then relax them. Clench your jaw or your mouth, your lips, hold tight for ten seconds, and then relax . Take a deep breath, hold ten seconds, and exhale slowly. It is also vital that you begin to identify what is going on at the time you become aware of the stress:

- Being too busy is one creator of stress.
- Conflict is a creator of stress.
- Finances can create stress.
- Wanting a drink or drug creates stress.

All of these stressors can be associated with your multiple roles. Only when you make the connection between the awareness of the stress and the cause of the stress can you begin to initiate the changes necessary to reduce it. Telling yourself you won't talk about or feel the stress only allows it to continue to control you.

Longer-term stress management can be strengthened by exercise, meditation, yoga, and multiple other methods. Low-cost courses are often offered by community agencies. Self-help books are abundant in libraries and bookstores, and almost every woman's magazine has an article on stress reduction. All of these can give new ways of thinking and acting.

Changing Roles and Relationships

For many of us, one of the most stressful yet important and exciting roles that we might want to change or at least modify is that of mother. As we said in the previous chapter on self-image, improving our relationship with our children improves our self-image. Unfortunately, in the midst of our addiction we did not always carry out the mother role in the way we wanted. In changing roles and relationships and reducing stress, it can be exciting to think of the role of mother within the framework of the loving relationship we want with our children. As we said earlier, healthy, empowering roles and relationships are based on mutual respect, honesty, and understanding. They recognize the potential and the essence of the other person. They give us a sense of courage and an ability to put our caring into actions. To think of the role of mother and the parent-child relationship in this way says, "I can be creative in this role. I respect you. I will be honest with you. I will work to understand you (your needs, feelings, fears). I recognize you as an individual." This mutually empowering relationship reframes the mother-child relationship in an inspiring way. It gives the courage to be the adult and to be respectful of the uniqueness of this precious relationship.

The addiction has also devastated the marriage relationship in many cases. The partner is hurt, angry, and afraid. In his general book about marriage, *The Seven Principles for Making Marriage Work* (see References), John Gottman says that most marriages end not because of an affair or money problems but rather because the partners have not taken care of the relationship. That goes about a hundred times over for relationships in marriages of addicted women. We have not taken care of the relationship! The drug took priority over and over again. Why should he believe things will be different this time? We've promised it before. And sadly, more often than not, he has left the relationship. You are there with your kids and the addiction, pretty much alone.

But if he is there in your recovery, gently share your new awareness of the stressors of your roles, of the changes you need to make to reduce the challenges to your recovery. The changes you are making might be very frightening to your partner. But as noted before, "If nothing changes, nothing changes." Begin to talk; ask for what you need to remain in recovery. Ask for help so you can get to a meeting, to take a class. Talk about your fear of relapse. Begin to listen! What are his concerns? What does *he* need? Begin to risk talking about your emotions in a way that acknowledges his emotions, fears, anxieties. Help create the atmosphere of a mutual relationship. Begin to talk about your hopes and dreams—what is important to you in this new life. Ask about his hopes and dreams for this new life. Listen. Talk. Feel. Trust.

And if you are not involved in a sexual relationship (as you move into recovery) don't initiate one! Most counselors will instruct women new to recovery not to move into a new sexual relationship with a "significant other" for at least a year. It's not that we are opposed to sex! But when we were addicted, we often confused sexual relations with intimacy. It is important to work on our self-discovery before we engage in the hard work of an intimate sexual relationship.

Changing Roles and Career

Another role that adds stress and might need to be modified or changed can be our choice of careers outside the home—the ones we get paid for. Some theories of stress indicate that we create stress to give ourselves a sense of importance and excitement. Examine your job, and decide what real stress it creates and what stress you create within it.

If a career fits with the role we want for our new life of recovery, it is satisfying and exciting. However, if we begin to be aware of stress at work that creates a desire for our drug, we are at risk. What causes you stress in your job? How do you know? Do the stress and your response to it set you up for relapse? We thought we could do it on our own...we could do it all. We didn't pay attention to the messages our body was giving us. We returned to our old patterns. We didn't make the awkward phone call. We didn't ask for help. We didn't make the hard decisions. *Sobriety lost its priority.*

If part of the change that needs to occur for your recovery is a career change, then the power of healthy relationships and the courage those relationships give us can be a great place to start. What woman has a job you would like to have? Call her up. Make an appointment. Tell her you would like an informational interview. Go talk with her. How did she get there? People love to talk about themselves. What job would be satisfying and exciting for you? What did you always want to be "when you grew up"? Can you begin a plan to get there? It starts with a plan. It starts with small steps. Ask yourself these questions:

- Do you need to get your GED?
- Do you need to improve your reading skills?
- Do you need to get a driver's license?
- Do you need to get food stamps?
- Do you need legal advice?
- Do you need to finish that college degree?
- Do you need to improve your interview skills?
- Do you need better time management skills?
  Money management skills?
- Where can you get help with some of these steps?

Look up community services listings in the phone book. It's a listing in the front: Community Service Numbers. There are state and local agencies for just about anything. Yes, it will take some energy and courage, but you are competent to pursue your goals. Maybe your dreams seem totally out of reach, but the truth is you *can* get there. Again, this is not a book of prescriptions of "how to get there," but I believe that naming the dream and identifying the steps in the process of attaining that dream give you excitement and energy—a new way of being. Take the first step. Being on the way in your career can reduce the stress. The dreams and the steps to reach them become an integral part of your recovery.

Changing Roles and Fun

A further way to reduce stress and create excitement is to start having fun...new fun that isn't related to the addiction. By now the addiction really isn't fun anymore, is it? Here, we are talking about fun related to the kinds of mature, adult roles and relationships women are motivated to have. As women, we all like to talk. Call a friend or Mom or sister. Maybe go to a movie but then talk later. Of course, we don't just want to talk. We want to be heard. We want to be validated. Fun for women is about relationships built on being heard, a shared experience, truth, honesty. A place to start having fun is with a woman friend…a friend who validates you and your struggle, a friend who listens, a friend with whom you laugh. Were there times before the addiction when you laughed so hard you wet your pants? I bet you were talking with a girlfriend. Can you imagine having that again? How? With whom do you laugh now?

Also, children are great resources to relearn how to have fun. Simply take them to a park, go down the slide after them, ride the merry-go-round. Did you like to ice skate or roller skate? Take your children, or borrow a kid from a friend. Laugh at your awkwardness. After all, how many years has it been? Go to the library, get a book they love, and play into it with them. Pretend, create magic, tell spooky stories. Find a big empty refrigerator box, and climb into it with them. Is it a spaceship? An airplane? A train? Where do they want to go? Where do you want to go? Whom do they want to go with them? What makes that person special? Whom do you want to go with you? What makes that person special?

Learn with them about a school project. It's not just about your "responsibility" as a parent; it is about your ability to respond: "response-ability." Where will your daughter learn about healthy fun? Where will she learn about her choices of roles? Where will your son learn about the roles, responsibilities, and relationships that healthy women want that also help him be healthy? For example, a woman who runs a halfway house speaks proudly of her daughter who recently was talking of career choices at school and said, "I want to do what my mom does. She helps other women turn their lives around." What a testimony to recovery!

Girls watch and learn.

Changing Roles by Reshaping

A further way to create the excitement of change is really no change at all, but rather a reshaping in the way we think. Celebrate this different sense of yourself—this competent, powerful woman. Celebrate in the new plan, a new way of thinking about the roles and relationships we are reshaping.

Anne Morrow Lindbergh in *Gift From the Sea* talks about this reshaping. She encourages women to reduce stress by reframing how they think about their daily tasks. She suggests women take the clutter from their lives to find a balance between solitude and community. She says it takes a simplicity of living to retain a true awareness of life. She also says that a woman can best find herself by losing herself in some kind of creative activity. What is your creative gift? Did it get lost in the addiction? How can you find it again?

Change and Recovery

Remaining in recovery takes creativity and courage. Every day you make decisions that take courage to step out of the old patterns, to risk something you know in your gut will strengthen this connection in relationship.

Consider Claire, who came to the retreat three days after being robbed. She shared her fears, her sense of vulnerability with women she didn't know, "Because if I am going to get anything out of this day, you have to know where I am."

Sheila came to the retreat with friends. She shared that her husband died six months after she entered recovery, leaving her with two teenagers. "I learned I could do things I never dreamed I could do. The most important one was not to take a drink. My new friends help me with this. "

Judith was very quiet all day. At the end of the day she said,

"This was one of the most courageous things I have done. I came by myself. I didn't know any of you."

Each of these women came with a personal need to connect. It was not easy to walk into a room and share with a group of strangers. But each woman knew she had to do something differently in her life to make progress in her recovery...to *transform* her life. We risk, we talk, we feel, we trust.

SUSTAIN

This recovery process takes a very long time, the rest of our lives. Our roles, responsibilities, and relationships are changing very slowly. To *sustain* recovery we take this creativity and courage of changed roles and relationships into our spiritual lives. We are not just adding a number of days or weeks or even years to our process of recovery. We are developing and growing. We become aware of the new shape of our lives—a new creation. We really are "becoming." We are a new creation. We have an awareness of the larger creation around us. In addition to a new shape to our lives, this new creation, there is a new presence in our lives—a sense of blessing.

Gradually we begin to take in the truth of this blessing. This truth molds our roles, responsibilities, and relationships beyond our simple transforming and into a sense of the sacred. We begin to recognize there is a sacredness in our roles, responsibilities, and relationships. The truth of this sacredness brings our daily lives into the mystery of faith. Maybe we don't even know what faith is or what faith means to us now. Maybe we haven't considered it for years. But little by little as we begin to recognize the gift of recovery, we begin to sense the grace that is being given to us simply because we are loved. Being blessed changes everything.

New Creation

There is a young woman I talk with periodically who fights the boredom in her roles, responsibilities, and relationships. She wants more excitement, more fulfillment. She dreams of running away and joining the Air Force, but with two young boys and a husband she really won't be able to do that. She struggles to see the laundry, the meals, the play as sacramental. And so she prays, "You are present, Gracious God, in the whole of my life, in the small tasks and in the big events; help me always to be aware of your presence and open to your purpose."

The small tasks and the big events are the responsibilities and the relationships of all those roles. Can you begin to become aware of those responsibilities and relationships as sacramental? Do you drive the kids to and from school? How do you use that time? Does everyone have his or her own iPod playing, or is there time to reflect on everyone's conversations or fights or listen to the kids' conversations with their friends? My daughter-in-law talks about her delight in being the take-home mom for the school carpool. She gets to listen to her twelve-year-old son and friends chatter about the goings-on at school that day. "I get to hear the excitement, the laughter, the gossip. I would never learn all that if I simply asked him how his day was once he came home." She experiences this awareness of the sacred gift. A school bus driver asked a group of parents, "Do you know who your kid had an argument with today? Do you know who she has a crush on? I do!" Listening is a sacred activity.

In so many ways children show us the sacredness in everyday creation. They have a wonderful capacity for living in the present moment. The wonder of a child stooping to look at a furry caterpillar. The joy of a child learning to ride a bike. The delight of the first snowfall. My uncle tells of taking his grandson to watch a sunset on the California coast. As the fireball set below the horizon the child turned and asked, "Does it do this every day?" Wonder is a sacred gift of children. Wonder is a sacred gift of recovery.

Very, very slowly we bring in the wonder and the sanctity of the day. We gain awareness of where we met God in this day. Maybe it was the clerk at the checkout line who gave a smile rather than a frown. Maybe it was a friend who had the courage to ask, "How's your recovery going?" Putting children to bed can be a blessed, sacramental time. Instead of asking our child, "How was your day?" we could ask, "Where did you meet God today?" Maybe God was in a bright red leaf, maybe in a friend who helped, maybe in a person who seemed sad. It teaches our child to share the wonder. It teaches each of us to be more aware of God's presence.

An awareness of this presence continues our journey to knowing we are blessed by God. In experiencing this blessedness we know God sees us as unique, special, and precious. It is not something we do. It is God's gift to us. Sometimes it is difficult to accept that we are blessed. Being blessed or receiving a blessing is more than an affirmation. An affirmation is often a word of praise or appreciation. When we receive a blessing it allows us to hear that we belong to a loving God. He will always be with us and guide us in every step of our lives.

Silence

How can we hear and claim the blessing? To hear the blessing we need to find the silence. Finding a place of silence is not isolation. It is not loneliness. It is not procrastination. It is finding a quiet place to hear your inner heart, to hear the voice of love. To feel the brightness within.

You may be thinking, "With all I have to do how on earth does she think I'm going to find a time and place of quiet!" What I am suggesting is that our addictions created noise and chaos in the world around us and in our heads. Can we now reclaim some time of quiet to hear his blessing? Isn't that what we are yearning for—a blessing that says we belong to a loving God? We are not alone in this. He will guide us. Take the time to hear the blessing.

To claim our blessedness we also need to be attentive to presence in the blessings other people give us. We often brush off these blessings. "Oh, it was nothing." But brushing off these blessings is not being humble. Brushing off these blessings is being careless of the gift we are given. Blessings are all around us. For example, a relative called recently to ask for my support. Her beloved cat had died. What a blessing that she called me. She chose me. The most meaningful blessings are words that tell us we are important to someone and also words of gratitude, encouragement, and love that people share with us. They remind us of the God who chose us.

We have to choose if we want to live in the place of being blessed, day by day and sometimes moment by moment. When we place our recovery firmly with God, we'll know the blessing and feel his presence.

Passing on the Blessing

If we feel blessed, it is easy to pass the blessing on. Passing on the blessing becomes part of each role and each relationship. If we feel our own blessedness, we can say good things to others about their lives and their beings. It comes naturally. When we are in the addiction, all we see is darkness. When we know we are blessed we sense light, joy, and power. We are given the words to bless others. When we become aware of our blessing and ultimately being God's daughter, it means God's love is there fresh and new each morning.

Do you awaken each morning with awe of the creation of a new day? Is the daily cycle of sunrise and sunset a symbol of your hope and of God's majesty? Many prayers have an inspirational way of drawing our attention to the wonder of morning, noon, and night. Here are just a few:

If I ascend to heaven, you are there; if I make my bed in
Sheol, you are there.

PSALM 139

A promise God will be there through all of the struggle...even if I choose to use again...to "make my bed in hell"—I am chosen and blessed.

When I look at your heavens, the work of your fingers,
the moon and the stars that you have established;
what are human beings that you are mindful of them,
mortals that you care for them?

PSALM 8:3–4

Where will I stand in awe of God's love today?

The tradition of daily prayer gives rhythm and creation to our lives. Morning prayer reminds us of our need to recommit ourselves to this miracle of change in our inmost selves. Prayer in the evening calls us to surrender our worries and anxieties of the day. It is a surrender to the God who invites us to share our lives with him and who longs to surround the darkness of the night with his all-encompassing peace. Release the day. Give it to God, and let God bring on the quiet. Then, even falling asleep becomes sacred.

The LORD *has been mindful of us; he will bless us.*

PSALM 115:12

Finding scriptural passages and meditative prayers that speak to our fears and anxieties is a way to center and *sustain* our recovery in a relationship with God. It begins a conversation with God. We begin to feel his calming, gentle presence. In the next chapter on communication we will talk further about this conversation with God.

Things to *Think About*

1. *What roles and responsibilities and relationships do you most enjoy?*
2. *Which cause you the most stress?*
3. *How will you get laughter back in your life?*
4. *What would it be like to let go of the fear that goes with addiction? To feel God's gentle presence?*

CHAPTER 3

I: Ineffective communication

Sandy, a client for several years, called and asked for an emergency appointment. She entered the office, offered a tight smile, and started the conversation. "I got a phone call yesterday morning about 7 AM. The woman on the other end said, 'This is Jan Newcomb.' The name sounded only vaguely familiar so I said, 'Yes?' She said, 'You probably don't remember me, but I need to tell you that I have been your husband's girlfriend for 15 years.'" Sandy paused, swallowed, and then continued, "This Jan person went on saying something like, 'He always said he wouldn't leave you until the kids were grown, but they're all grown now and I want to know what he plans to do.' She continued for a while reminding me of when she and I had met and telling me of some of the times he and she had been together. I was speechless. Finally, she said, 'So what do you have to say?' I stupidly said, 'I don't have anything to say' and hung up." Sandy took a longer pause and said, "I confronted him last evening. He got really pale and his hands clearly shook when I recounted the conversation. But he denied she was his girlfriend or that there was 'anything like what you and I have.'"

Sandy stopped and took a sip of water. There were no tears. I waited. She looked at me and said, "You know, I think I knew all along. There were times I wondered but I was afraid to ask." Sandy then recounted clues that now had become clear—repetitive trips he had taken that really didn't fit with his job; times he came home late, had not wanted dinner, was distracted, and had flimsy excuses; times he smelled of a different aftershave than he used at home. She was silent for a few minutes and then she said something very significant, something that is often at the root of our ineffective communication, "*I didn't know what I knew.*"

"Not knowing what we know" is at the core of this chapter. It is about "not knowing what we know" about ourselves, our own stories, our own addictions, about being in relationship. And "not knowing what we know" about God, in prayer.

WHAT IS COMMUNICATION?

Communication, both ineffective and effective, is a much broader topic than we may have once thought. We have talked about communication in both the chapter on self-image and the chapter on traditional roles as communication related to those topics. In this chapter we will talk about specific communication techniques, specific gender aspects of communication, a critical feature of communication we often miss—listening. We will also talk about our communication with God—prayer.

Years ago, in discussions about communication we talked about things like differences between assertive and aggressive language, verbal and nonverbal cues. Those are important parts of communication, but there is so much more. Communication, especially women's communication, is about the way we come to know ourselves, the way we come to know the world, and the way we communicate the truth of that knowing.

Communication also includes how we make sense of what we have experienced. We watch. We listen. We learn. We come to know our own story. We then work to find our voice, to share what we know. We ask ourselves, what is our truth? And we do all this within supportive and affirming relationships. Within these relationships we find our voice and begin the "talking" that we usually think of as communication. But before the talking comes silence, watching, and listening. It is only then, after we watch and listen, that we find our own authentic voice, that we know the truth about ourselves and we begin to feel our core sense of being alive.

This new way of envisioning communication is how we move from

- *Name*—making sense of what we have experienced and knowing our own story to
- *Transform*—finding our voice within ourselves and in relationship; and
- *Sustain*—creating communication with God

NAME

Women who grew up in chaotic and unpredictable homes are often silent women. That is, we have difficulty identifying what real truth is for us, to whom and what authority we should pay attention, and to whom we should listen for wisdom. We have difficulty figuring out who we are, how to interact with others, and what control we have over life events. These descriptions apply to many women with addictions who are in recovery and many who are not there yet. Women with addictions are silent women—women who grew up with the "don't talk...don't feel...don't trust" rules in chaotic and unpredictable homes.

Nancy remembers it this way. "I had no voice as a child. I was a runner. When there was trouble, I ran to the woods until my mom went to sleep. This was when I was about nine or ten. I was never allowed to express an opinion. She often said I was stupid and ugly. You agreed with her or else. If you disagreed it was painful. She would beat me, throw things. Once when I ran outside she threw an iron through the window after me." Nancy became one of the "silent women." She feared voicing her opinion would bring physical pain and emotional estrangement. She learned to not talk, not feel, not trust. Early on she used marijuana and alcohol to calm the fear and escape the pain. Sound familiar?

Early Years—Words as Weapons

When a young girl lives in a chaotic and unpredictable environment, she experiences constant fear of an eruption. Speechless and numbed, she can't risk an exploration of what might be happening. Her questions are judged as "talking back" and disrespectful. The parent expects the child to read his or her mind. She is never asked to explain her own thinking. Instead, parents yell. And all too often, parents become violent. So the child withdraws, runs for cover, and "becomes silent." With no trust or order in her world, she is unable to develop her own ability to hear and to know.

As we described in the Self-image and Traditional Roles sections, a little girl's family commands the major role in her development. In this chapter we see the impact of the family on the girl's ability to communicate effectively—or not. Haven't you read stories and testimonials of "successful" families where everyone sits down for dinner and has meaningful discussions? In those families children and parents dialogue and even respectfully argue about current events and morals and religion. Children have a right to their own opinions. Listening and having conversations with others is valued. For healthy families this type of communication becomes a necessary part of their mutual relationship. It helps develop the child's own ability to think, to form their own opinions, and to hear their own inner voice. It is how a child develops her own thought process. And didn't you wonder, "Who *are* these families?" They are certainly not families with addiction issues.

Little Girls

In earlier chapters we talked of how it is typical for a little girl to stay close to mother and learn her role by watching—and listening. She watches how mother interacts with her, and she listens to how mother interacts with others. In a healthy home, a mother uses communication to draw her daughter out. Mother seems to understand that, in hearing what her daughter has to say, the daughter develops her own thinking and her own understanding of her thinking. When mother genuinely asks, "Tell me what you think about this. How is that for you? Help me understand how you came to that conclusion. What do you think your friend is feeling?" and having asked these questions, the mother really listens to the answers, her daughter then develops her own truth and understanding of reality.

In addition to a young girl's time with her mother, playtime with other children is essential to making meaning of her own experience. In play with others, a child learns to converse, learns to listen to others, and learns to hear her own voice. Little girls in play are a delight to watch. When I stop outside my granddaughter's bedroom and listen to her talk with her dolls I get to know how she views the world. Talk of birthday parties and pony rides and playing school let me know the world is safe for her. Listening to her play with friends shows me how she negotiates, settles arguments, and knows the power of her voice. One of our favorite activities together is to draw pictures and then tell each other the story about the pictures. What a joy to validate her ideas, her choices, and her voice. Asking the next questions such as, "What makes you think that? What makes her feel that way? What do you think might happen here?" yields responses that help her hear her own thinking, to find her voice. She is very young, but she wants a diary "with a lock." I smile with delight. Her inner voice has value to her, and it is hers to protect.

One day she and I were watching a Disney movie about dogs left in Antarctica when the owners had to be evacuated. Lexi had seen the movie several times. It was my first viewing. Being a bit of a softie by nature, I became tearful when one of the dogs was dying. Lexi looked at me and in a very concerned voice said, "It's OK, Grandma. He didn't really die in real life. I saw him on the Disney Channel and he is just fine." She brings me a tissue. Her world is safe. It makes sense to her. She can care for others.

In contrast, little girls raised in chaotic homes are given frightening words and rules and roles that damage healthy relationships and silence their voices. Sometimes forever.

Adolescents

As we have noted in earlier chapters, adolescence is a critical time for development of self-knowledge, self-image, and voice. Often it is a time, even in normal development, in which a girl's sense of self and voice frequently become submissive. Culture tells her she must defer to others' needs and desires if she wants to be in relationship.

If she is to learn how to develop healthy give-and-take relationships it becomes essential for her to establish the part of herself that is in relationship with peers and especially boys. Too often in an effort to stay in the relationship she begins to lose touch with her powerful part—the part of her *self* that has an ability to be an active, equal partner in the relationship. She begins to not say what she feels or thinks if it might mean being left out of her clique or losing her boyfriend.

Adolescent girls in families with addiction issues also often begin to experience a further break in relationship within the family. This break can show itself in significant anger in the mother-daughter relationship. Because of the amount of abuse and violence in families with addiction, this is one scenario that might occur. The daughter has had a close tie with the mother, sometimes as confidante, sometimes as protector. As the daughter reaches adolescence, she becomes aware of the emotional and/or physical abuse the mother has tolerated. Because she has had little experience in making sense of her world, she is unable to look at the larger picture of the mother's situation. Maybe in reality mother believes she can't support the children if she tells him to leave. Maybe mother fears for their safety if she leaves. Maybe mother sees no options. The daughter has not been taught how to think beyond the rules and the role she herself has been assigned. In adolescence she becomes angry at the mother for "taking it for all these years." The adolescent daughter hears no sense of power or empowerment from her mother.

For example, I recently heard a very educated, scholarly woman describe her mother's alcoholism. "They always had their martinis in the afternoon. These days, we would call my mother an alcoholic. She really had that change of personality. Her anger would emerge, and God help whoever was in her line of fire. I was to be voiceless and selfless. It was all very 'crazy making,' and I emerged a raging neurotic. I escaped into books and achievement. It took years for me sort it all through, to get some sense of where her anger came from."

A Native American adult student of mine spoke frequently in counseling of her abusive husband. She saw no escape even though she clearly saw the damage it was doing to her children, whose behavior was out of control. She knew that her husband's family would disown her if she pressed further charges. This would be an enormous cultural loss. The police officer who frequently responded to her 911 calls encouraged her to leave her husband. One day she called me around 6 AM. She said, "I am sending the children to school with their essential things in their backpacks. I will come to nursing class, and then the kids and I will go the shelter this afternoon. I will call the police and have him arrested.

Last night after he hit me and my son, my daughter asked, 'Are all men as bad as Daddy?' I can't let her think this is all there is."

In almost all families with addictions and violence, such as the women above, the issues are kept as secrets. That's what the rules are for. The family has to look OK to the outside world. And it needs to be acknowledged that even lots of "normal" families have secrets—secrets such as financial problems, physical illness, unexpected pregnancies. It's just that families with addiction don't acknowledge there is a secret even to themselves. It is the elephant in the living room, and nobody talks about it. As my friend says, "It's crazy making." We doubt our gut. "I shouldn't be so scared when he yells, when he leaves, when she cries. (Don't feel.) I can't let anyone know. (Don't talk.) They would think I'm nuts. After all, he is charming when he is at church. I must be the one who is crazy. (Don't trust them or myself.)" And the voice within becomes silent. "I won't think about it. I'll lose myself in books or school—or I'll keep so busy I'll feel like I have control. I'll buy more stuff. I'll do drugs. Or throw up. Or sex."

It is up to us as recovering women to find our voices, to break the rules of *In*effective communication, the rules of don't talk, don't feel, don't trust, and to move into our adult roles with healthy, effective communication. Our lives and the lives of those we love depend on it.

TRANSFORM

Finding the voice within requires incredible courage. As we said, finding the voice within is about listening as much as talking. Our listening requires attentiveness and watching. By watching and listening to others, we begin to sense a difference between other women's reality and what we were taught as reality. With that attentiveness and watching and listening comes discovery—discovery of differences and similarities with what we thought was truth. We move into exploring a new reality, a personal truth through communication first with ourselves and then in connection with others. Ultimately, we move into a way of knowing that is authentic and connected. *Transformative.*

Pay Attention to Your Gut

As Nancy said, she ran. She ran away physically, and she ran away emotionally. When she disagreed with her mother or voiced her own opinion , her mother responded with physical violence or words as weapons. To have her own voice was to be told by parents and teachers, her "external authorities," she was stupid and crazy. She came to believe the external authorities were right. She shut down her feelings and her belief in herself, even when her gut told her maybe they were wrong. (Don't feel.)

Remember Sandy, who said, "I didn't know what I knew." She, too, had not listened to her gut. She reflected that, when there were contradictions between what she sensed and what her husband had said, she had asked him about the discrepancies. He discounted her thoughts and feelings. When she had asked about the pattern of trips out of town, he said it couldn't be done by teleconference. When she saw a phone bill with multiple long-distance phone calls to a place where they had no friends, he said the calls must have been placed by one of their kids. The kids said they didn't have any friends there either. The bills disappeared. She accepted his explanations though her gut told her differently.

Ineffective Communication and Relationships

Growing up in chaotic families, children learn how to stay out of relationships while they act and even think they are in relationships. I shared this theory with Sandy as she worked on connecting the dots between the patterns of her family when she was a child (don't talk) and the patterns of her own marriage. Her eyes widened. "It wasn't just him who wasn't in the relationship, was it? I wasn't in the relationship either. I wasn't willing even to tell him what I was thinking or how I felt about this stuff. I just asked and then dropped it. I wasn't willing to talk about anything that would make either of us uncomfortable." (Don't talk. Don't trust.)

For Nancy and Sandy the realization of the disconnect between the rules they had been taught and the feeling in their gut came from different sources. But both of them had to listen and watch in order to heal. Nancy first heard the disconnect in the outpatient substance abuse group therapy. She had said absolutely nothing in the groups. I thought she was closed to the entire process. Later, when she returned to individual counseling, she said she had just wanted to blend in, to not be noticed. (Here she was the Lost Child.) But she said that when she attended the group she heard others acknowledge some of the same situations she had experienced, and they said they were angry. They raged. They cried. They didn't accept those situations as normal or valid. She heard them being appalled at circumstances she had accepted as part of normal family life. She heard them support each other. She watched and listened. She began to paint.

Sandy felt the disconnect between the explanations she had been willing to accept from her husband and the reality presented by his girlfriend "like someone hit me in the head with a board....Where on earth have I been? I've heard other women tell this story and wondered how naive can they be?" Sandy did not see herself as a naive person. In an effort to heal she was willing to explore how she had come to be the woman who dropped the subject rather than confront. She knew she was not that woman in her professional role. How was she that woman in her marriage relationship.? She was willing to explore the messages she had heard in her chaotic childhood home, to look at her parents' relationship and what she had learned from their examples, and to examine other meaningful relationships. She realized she had been told by her parents she was lucky to have the security provided by her husband; she was lucky to have his good disposition; and, if there was ever trouble between them, she was probably the cause. She had learned to deny there was a problem. Her silence avoided any chaos. Her silence removed any threat of disruption of "the perfect marriage." Her silence maintained her role as caretaker of the relationship, and her silence kept her out of the work of relationship.

The Work of Therapy

Both Nancy and Sandy did some hard work in individual and group therapy. They used therapy to connect the dots. When I asked them later what was useful for them in the therapy, they were able to name some important things. Their insights are worth considering as you think about finding a counselor or group to help guide your own healing. They listened to others—and not just because they wanted to see if the stories were like their stories but ultimately because they began to care for the other women in the group. They could empathize with the feelings of emptiness and fear. They found themselves thinking about and worrying about other group members between meetings. They said in therapy they were able to begin to talk about themselves. They could express their feelings, reflect on those feelings, and bring up memories without feeling self-conscious. They didn't have to think about choosing their words carefully. Others would help them clarify their thoughts and words. They said this was an active part of their healing process. They saw therapy as supportive and candid. They said they were able to name the problems, look at the patterns in their lives, and connect the past experiences with what was happening in their lives at the present time. They were able to begin to try out new ways of using their voices...to have their communication reflect their feelings in a constructive way and in relationships. They began to listen to "the still small voice within," to break through their own denial, to trust their gut, and to confront their addiction with a new openness.

Our Gut, Our Denial, and Our Addiction

What has "the still small voice within" been telling us about our addiction? Without a doubt it's been saying, "You're in big trouble!"

Did we hear it?

It has been telling us this is not the life we want.

We tell it to shut up.

It has been telling us we need to do something differently.

We say it isn't so bad.

The "don't" rules and the role(s) we have assumed keep us in denial of how much we are using, how it is screwing up our lives, how it is affecting those we love. If we can begin to listen to the voice within, we hear the contradictions.

I heard the voice in the night that cried, "What am I going to do about this?"

But I also heard the other voice that told me to have one more—I deserved it.

We hear the voice within that says, "Why am I doing this?"

But we also hear the other voice that says, "You aren't so bad. You haven't been arrested. You got home safely. You know how much fun it is to get high. You don't want to give that up."

We hear and latch onto the friend who says, "Well, we just all drank a lot that night."

We tell ourselves, "The doctor gave me this. It has to be OK even if I take more than what the prescription says."

But in time if we are open, we hear the contradictions. We begin to watch and listen. We notice the contradictions between the denial voice and the feeling in the gut. We begin to hear the still small voice within that says, "Yeah, I got home without an accident this time, but that was pure luck. I could easily have killed someone." Or, "I needed that Percocet for my pain, but is stealing it worth the guilt, the fear?"

When we begin to pay attention and listen to the contradictions we open to a new reality. We open to the experience of a changing self. We begin to really hear the voice within, our true self. We begin to reflect and think about the contradictions. As Sandy said, "It's like watching a movie and knowing something the heroine doesn't know. She makes a choice, and we can hardly stand it because we know she's going to get screwed." In our recovery we must stop, watch, listen to that voice within. We need to stop screwing ourselves. We need to hear our inner truth.

New Reality of Old Experiences

The opinions of others often make it difficult to separate our true voice from the other voices. As we said in Chapter 1, the messages and voices from our past remain in our heads for a long time, and we spend a lot of our adult time in discussions with nonexistent people. Again, it is helpful to be aware of the conversations we have with people who "aren't there." Those conversations are not the small voice within that is our true voice. These "conversations in our head" can be ineffective communication if we stay stuck in hearing them as the truth. But listening to those conversations in our heads also can give us great insight into where our beliefs and experiences come from. Reflecting on those conversations and critiquing them gives wonderful self-knowledge. Who is talking? What are they saying? Have you heard that voice, that message before? What do you feel during the conversation? Taking all of this out of your head and writing it in a journal or just making notes to yourself is vital. It gives a place to start probing the world from a place inside of you.

Relationship With Others— Communication in Connection

"Knowing what we know" comes from listening to the voice within, separating that from the old voices and messages, and then having the courage to interact, dialogue, and check out our new awareness and information. We do this checking out in trustworthy relationships. Checking out the new knowledge in relationship is sometimes called *connected knowing*. Connected knowing happens in relationships that have equality and trust as their foundation. The goal is one of understanding. This connected knowing does not come from relationships that are distant and impersonal. It comes within relationships that foster give and take, respect, caring, and empowerment (*Women's Ways of Knowing*; see References).

The new knowledge blossomed inside Nancy when she talked about her paintings. The second group of paintings (after her own *Silent Scream*) she brought to show me were landscapes. The scenes were of quiet brooks, sheltering trees, exquisite flowers, church spires in quiet villages. In all her life experience of pain and trag-edy, in all the messages of rejection from others, there was a place deep inside of gentleness and stillness. We talked about what that place feels like. We talked about the contradictions. We talked about the process of painting as a way to be in those quiet places. We explored other ways to be in those quiet places. She began to feel the truth of her self.

Sandy's connected knowing came in a unique form of journaling. She resisted the suggestion of writing daily. She said she preferred reading rather than writing. She was reading voraciously on top-ics such as personal growth, self-help, marriage, parenting, and spirituality. She brought many quotes to therapy, and we would talk about their validity to her growth and healing—her connected knowing. She began to keep these quotes in a notebook and talked about her pleasure in rereading them time and time again. She would make her personal notes beside them.

Nancy now has about fifteen years of recovery behind her. It isn't the perfect abstinence some people define as recovery, but it is her growth in care and empowerment of herself and others. It is reflective of a strong process of recovery. She says she keeps a journal in her painting.

Sometimes the care and empowerment come in journaling and the stuff of everyday living and sometimes in the process of redefining the rules and roles. Of the everyday stuff, Nancy recently said she was still surprised when she can empower herself within her relationship with her husband. "Sometimes I find my voice with Johnny. To stand up for myself feels good. Just last week I told him to pick up his own clothes. I told him I wasn't going to do it anymore. The voice I heard inside my head told me I was angry every time I did it. Thirty-four years is long enough." She smiled. I also asked her how she found her voice in an incident at work. "I just decided not to take it anymore. One of my coworkers said I was stupid. I thought to myself, 'I'm not stupid. That's what my mom used to say, and I don't believe that anymore.'" Nancy is an evening custodian in an office building. She works with two other female custodians. There had been a series of incidents in which the other two custodians had been critical of her work, her attitude, and her breaks. In fact, Nancy was suspicious that the other two had "undone" some of her tasks. I encouraged her to document each incident by date, time, and what was said. As she expected, the other two custodians took their complaints to the supervisor. Nancy requested a joint meeting. Nancy brought "her voice" in the documentation and in her clear assertive language. "I am not stupid and they must stop using that language around me." The supervisor supported Nancy and her "voice."

An even more telling incident was in Nancy's ability to stand up to her entire family. In this incident, relating to an accusation of abuse involving two relatives, she exercised her voice and gave up her assigned roles of Scapegoat and Lost Child. A male relative had been accused of sexual abuse of a teenaged female cousin. (Now remember, Nancy had been raped and abused by family members her whole life. It would have been so easy to slip into judgment and the victim role.) In the old days, she had been the one accused of being at fault. But in this incident Nancy was able to step out of the family's pattern of judging and persecuting without clear information. She no longer automatically accepted the family's rush to judgment. She was able to watch, listen, critique, evaluate, and come to her own conclusion about the incident. She said, "I was alone in my support of Carl. It was a witch-hunt and I wasn't going to have any part of it, because it was wrong to judge him. It was what they used to do to me." Having her own thinking and gaining a voice gives Nancy the opportunity to step out of those assigned childhood roles. It allowed a family the opportunity to look at its pattern.

Family Communication

This whole business of watching and listening and finding our voice is a major part of how we heal in our recovery and how our families heal. It is how the patterns are recognized and interrupted. However, in recognizing the patterns and finding our voice within our families, it is practical to proceed with caution. Proceeding carefully is a way to take care of ourselves. If your family has been like those we have described as chaotic, your recovery may be very threatening to them. You are changing. You are shifting the balance in the mobile, and they may fear it will all come crashing down. Your parents or siblings may not be ready to hear your voice, and you may worry that they will reject your truth. Even your spouse and children may be suspicious of your emerging new self. Remember, healing connections are ones where there is equality, intimacy, trust, and safety. The goal of effective communication in healing connections is toward interaction and dialogue, not debate and arguing. Your family may not be ready to acknowledge the disease of addiction and how it has affected them. *But you have acknowledged it.* You are learning your own truth. Go slowly and carefully with family. Work with a therapist or mentor. You own what happened to you, and you are the one in the process of healing.

Healing Language, Empowerment, and Gender Differences

We own how our addiction affected ourselves and others. Healing is about hearing that truth in our own inner voice and sharing that in an authentic relationship. It is also about the words and language we use. It is about taking our healing and using it in the care of others. And it is about acknowledging the differences in how women and men communicate.

As in the Traditional Roles section when the discussion focused on marital relationships, a few ideas were suggested and reference was made to the many books written on the subject. However, here are a few thoughts or concepts that seem particularly pertinent to our focus on a gender-specific approach to communication.

"I" Statements

The particular words we use are powerful. Using "I" statements and assertive versus aggressive language are techniques of effective communication we have been teaching for years. They are still important tools, especially as we take responsibility for our disease, the behaviors we display, and the new emerging self. Use of "I" statements expresses our feelings and thoughts, and they are less likely to be critical than "you" statements. They make the person listening less defensive than a statement that starts with an accusatory "you."

Listen to the difference: "You haven't done a thing to help me all day" versus "I am feeling so stressed with all I have to do. I need some help."

We need to learn assertive language that expresses our needs and asks for our requests without stepping on the other person or making that person "wrong." Again, watching and listening are great ways to become aware of the differences between "I" statements and "you" statements and assertive versus aggressive communication. It is important to understand that "I" statements cannot simply be about getting our feelings out there. These statements have to be made as we think about the relationship and how our statement is going to build connection. Connection and understanding are the goals. It's also just fine to hear ourselves make a "you" accusatory statement and then say, "Whoops! Let me say that another way." It shows we are listening to ourselves and learning.

MALE RELATIONAL DREAD

It is vital, also, for women to acknowledge the differences we have with men in connections, relationships, and the language involved. It is not unusual for men to see a request to explore the connections, to deepen the relationship as a demand or criticism.

In an example of these differences, the Stone Center, when it researched women's relational theory, coined the term "male relational dread." I was somewhat amused by these concepts when I first read them, but more and more as I worked in couples' therapy I saw them as the valid truth of men's experience in relationship. Several concepts explored in male relational dread give us insight into men's experience. When we women find our voices, use new language, and crave healing in deeper, more connected relationships, we must consider their perspective.

The male relational dread concepts were developed when men in groups were asked to talk about "the relationship" with their wives or girlfriends. The men said that when their significant other started a discussion about "the relationship" they often felt

1. *The inevitability of disaster. Nothing good can come of my going into this; it's just a question of how bad it will be before it's over;*
2. *Timelessness. It will never be over; an eternity would be too brief;*
3. *Damage. The damage will be immense, and irreparable.*

STEPHEN BERGMAN, FROM "WORK IN PROGRESS"

These are only a few of the concepts explored by the Stone Center, but they highlight some very basic differences between men's and women's expectations of talking about the relationship. Generally, we women love to talk about the relationship. Apparently, many men dread it. We need to be attentive to our language and our expectations. Too often as women we think, "If he loved me he'd know I need this." Husbands, children, bosses are not mind readers. It has nothing to do with love. It has to do with their different gender perspectives and with our own responsibility—"response-ability." Our responsibility is to identify our feelings and needs, listen to their needs, find our voice, and express those needs and feelings within caring and empowering relationships.

Listening as Sacred

As we become empowered, we are more able to hear the voices of those we love. Listening is an essential part of empowering others. Real listening is sacred. It means caring for the other person in a deeply meaningful way. In most social conversations I find that I can ask another person, "How are you?" and the rest of the conversation is exclusively about their concerns, interests, or stressors. Very rarely do they ask how I am. When we were actively in the addiction we didn't want to listen. It was all about *me* and my priorities. In recovery, when we want to be in close connection, in a trusting relationship, we learn to listen. We begin to gain a sense of trust and faith in ourselves, in our ability to be in relationship, to care for and empower others. This communication in connection brings a joy and zest and energy to our recovery.

SUSTAIN

This joy and zest we feel as we listen and find our voice leads to an awareness of another voice within. This further voice conveys a longing for quiet, for stillness, for a deep sense of inner peace. We yearn for an inner gentleness we have not experienced for a long, long time. In *sustain* we discover a new and gentle communication with God. We practice this with a sense of sacred, and we risk an openness of our heart and life.

In her early recovery, Nancy struggled. She could stay away from the drugs and alcohol for a while, but it was more "hanging on by my fingernails" than any sense of peace. She would talk about the lifetime of abuse, about the death of her son. Then she described the deep emptiness inside. "It feels like a God hole." I encouraged her to pray, to use her true voice, her inner voice. She said, "I don't know how to pray....I wouldn't know what to say.... In fact I don't think he listens to people like me." It was then I suggested she talk with Joe, the pastoral counselor who had led discussions on spirituality in the outpatient program. Nancy told me those were really the only presentations she had liked. Nancy now credits much of her long-term recovery to the spiritual support, direction, and embrace of this pastoral counselor, Joe. Some months after Nancy had started meeting with Joe, she talked about a particularly difficult incident and her subsequent desire to drink. I asked her what she had done differently this time to not pick up. She said, "I prayed." And then I asked Joe to meet with me.

The following notes from my discussion with Joe opened an astonishing new personal perspective on prayer for me. Here's how Joe described prayer.

In a spiritual sense, in prayer we are talking about communicating with God. But what is prayer? The usual answer is talking with God. But there is a much deeper issue here. Who exactly is this God we are talking to? What is he like? Why bother with him? Indeed many would say that if prayer is communication with God, then it is ineffective because their prayers are never answered.

Perhaps it would be helpful to redefine prayer, but to do that we need to rethink our concept of God. To know who God is, we must listen to what he tells us about himself. He cares about us. As Henri Nouwen said, we are his beloved. He wants us to experience wholeness and health. He knows what we need even before we ask. He is more ready to give than we are to ask. He is not, however, a God who will force himself upon us. Given that definition of God, prayer can be thought of as "giving God permission to help." Prayer is coming to God with an open heart and open hands—asking and trusting him to involve himself in our lives so we can experience life in all its fullness and richness:

Trusting that he wants us to experience recovery.

Trusting that he will energize us toward recovery.

So to have effective communication with God is to give him permission to help us on our journey toward recovery. It

*is trusting that he cares for us and that he will most certainly
give us those gifts necessary for sobriety even if we can't
name them. Does that mean prayer is a magical thing? No.
Does that make God someone whom we can manage and
manipulate? No. It simply means that prayer is opening our
hearts and lives to God confident that he will quietly and
gently involve himself on our lifelong journey to recovery.*

Silence of Prayer

Joe spoke of "opening our hearts and lives to God." How do we
do that? Perhaps, it's simply by beginning to think about our relationship with God. We have formed a new life of recovery. We
have lifted out new ways of thinking about the destructive lessons
of those old rules and roles. We see communication as much more
than talking. We have begun to know the essence of communication as listening and connection.

A new creation has started to take shape. This new creation
makes us aware of this voice deep within us. The new voice asks
for inner peace. It asks for an open heart and open hands to know
God is with us in this journey. We begin with silence. We begin
with the intention to be open to hearing God's promise. He has
said we are in his blessing. How do we begin to hear the promise,
the blessing?

One way we begin to hear is by having some periods of quiet. We
might begin to hear by thinking of words of Dietrich Bonhoeffer,
a German theologian killed in a Nazi concentration camp. He was
not a Jew but was exterminated because he was involved in a plot
to assassinate Hitler. Bonhoeffer believed quiet is simply being held
by the promises of God. We are to be quiet at the start of the day
because God wants to have the first word, and we are to be quiet
before going to sleep because the last word also belongs to God.
Quiet is really nothing more than waiting and opening ourselves

to God's promise and blessing. A few moments before we bound out of bed, a few moments after we turn out our light at night. Quiet. Listening for God's promise (D. Bonhoeffer; see References).

Bonhoeffer also suggests that a more in-depth way we might begin this time of quiet is with a scripture reading. After the scripture reading we focus on one word or one phrase from that reading that speaks to us personally. A scriptural phrase that has touched my recovery deeply and I have used in my silence says God promises to release me "from the snare of the fowler" (Psalm 91). The snare of the fowler is a leather strap secured around a falcon's leg. The falcon cannot fly without the fowler or keeper releasing the leather strap. That is what addiction felt like for me. My ankle, my leg, and my whole being were trapped by the fowler's snare. The snare of the addiction kept me tethered, unable to do anything but frantically flap my wings in an effort to break loose. God's promise is that he will release me from that snare. This promise is heard in silent prayer. In this prayerful silence it is not necessary to say words or form sentences. We simply seek this relationship with God. We seek a new openness. We seek to be open to his word, his phrase, his promise, his freedom. This word penetrates our heart. It remains with us through the day.

To bring this promise with us through the day is a continuing part of the prayer. This is the prayer we utter from within when we are alone. It is a readiness and openness to receive God's promise— to accept it in our own personal situation, in our tasks, decisions, and temptations. We make it silently known to God. When I pray to "be released from the fowler's snare" I pray that God's promise is clear to me in what I will meet that day, that I will be able to manage it with his grace, and that I will feel his presence when I need his strength. It works in us throughout the day without our even being conscious of it.

When we enlarge this practice of silence and prayer to intercessory prayer, we think about people with whom we are in connection. Some may be our family; some may be friends and people at work, friends in recovery, or even those who cause stress in our lives. This part of prayer means nothing more than to bring this person into the presence of God, to see him or her as a person in need of grace. Too often when I pray I want to "fix it" and I want God to help me "fix it"—whatever "it" is. This is especially true if it involves someone I love deeply. Someone who may be in pain or distress. When I am able to place my prayer within an understanding of my communication with God, then my prayer simply brings this person into the presence of God. I pray that this person will know God's presence in their pain or distress. In this practice of silent prayer, I begin to have the deep sense of inner peace that feels like real recovery.

Things to *Think About*

1. *What do the old negative voices in your head say?*
2. *Practice listening to the differences between "I" statements and "you" statements in your own and others' conversations.*
3. *Take a few minutes of quiet and ask to be open to God's presence.*

CHAPTER 4

G: Grief and Loss

*A*ll of these recovery issues, Self-image, Traditional roles, Ineffective communication, and now Grief and loss, are central to opening ourselves to this new life of recovery. If we don't look carefully at these issues, they block our progress and make relapse more likely. Unexamined recovery issues interfere with our connections with ourselves, with those we love, and with God.

We have all encountered losses in our lives. Losses happen in our normal process of living. At one time, they may have been smaller losses such as a teenage romance, a bad grade in school, or a personal belonging. At other times there are more serious ones, such as losing a job or a good friend. Some of our losses might have been caused by our addiction, such as loss of a marriage, our financial credit, or even our freedom. We grieve them all.

In this chapter of Grief and Loss we first *name* our losses. Then we *transform* those losses through "grief work." We are able to *sustain* our recovery in a new understanding of forgiveness.

When we *name* the significant losses of our lives, we allow ourselves to consider the impact the loss had on us, the sadness we still carry, and the guilt and shame associated with a particular loss. The opportunity to identify the losses and examine the guilt and shame diminishes its control over our lives. This is the beginning of grief work for losses in our lives. Leaving our addiction behind is another kind of loss, in spite of the freedom this new recovery gives us. Women in recovery sometimes say they feel they have lost their "best friend." How does one replace a best friend?

Transform takes us through the stages of grief specifically focusing grief work related to our addiction. This work moves us closer to a deeper and stronger understanding of our life experience and its possible connection with our addiction. It's helpful to consider the usual stages of grief as we work through this and explore what we have accomplished in each stage, reminding ourselves that our life losses and our addiction losses are often intertwined. We also need to examine the incredible sense of guilt and shame often associated with loss.

Sustain explores how we move through the guilt and shame to experience a sense of acceptance of ourselves, and the wonder of the incredible love, mercy, and forgiveness of God.

Before we begin this discussion I'd like to share with you a very personal loss I experienced in my early recovery. The impact of that loss on my life, how it shaped my middle life, and how the grieving process shaped my recovery are essential to my sustained recovery and connection with God.

MY PERSONAL LOSS

When I was first in early recovery, I felt that remarkable exhilaration when I began to realize I have no control over my addiction but I do have control over my decisions. As I have said before, I delighted in the new freedom that I would no longer need to feel the guilt of driving drunk with the children in the car. I would no longer feel the embarrassment of drinking too much at a party, or the shame of being confronted at work. I went to self-help, heard stories like my own, and began to smile again. I enrolled in some graduate school courses, lost ten pounds, and thought I had my life back.

In June of that year, six months into my recovery, my twelve-year-old daughter was killed in a traffic accident. She was riding a minibike with her brother at a farm we were visiting in rural Pennsylvania. They crossed the country road at the end of the lane to ride in a neighboring field. She was hit and killed by a pickup truck driven by a man heading home for lunch. The tragedy was no one's fault. But my grief and loss/guilt and shame were overwhelming. I found no relief. At one level, I thanked God I was sober. I knew that if I had been drinking and had felt my thinking was foggy that morning, I probably would never recover. But on another level, the pain was unbearable. I could not share the intensity of the grief with anyone. The pain was physically palpable—in my chest, in my heart, and mostly in my soul. What could I have done differently that morning? Why didn't I remind her again to stay on our lane? A mother's main responsibility is to keep her children safe. I had failed as a parent. Overwhelming guilt. Overwhelming shame.

Over the next months I went through the motions of my daily activities, watched for her to come home after school, cried quietly in my room. I didn't attend self-help but I also didn't drink. But at Christmas time I picked up the first glass of champagne that came by on a tray. No plan to drink—just the tiger in the grass. Of course I thought I could handle it. It eased the pain a little. Nevertheless, within a few weeks I was back to buying the small bottle of wine and pouring it into the big one I now kept again in the refrigerator. (The small one was easier to hide in the trash.)

Fortunately I found my way back to recovery within a month, obtained a good therapist, and began to work my way through the grief and loss, guilt and shame. But that grief process continues even today, and it has to be part of my recovery every day. The loss, the guilt, and even the shame can still catch me if I deny it is part of my life. The recovery from addiction and the recovery from the loss of my daughter have to be held in my belief of God's love and grace, in his promise of his unfailing presence in my life.

Painful and Normal

I entered a graduate nursing program three months after my daughter's death. This had been planned before her death. Fortunately I was able to explore my "clinical" grief within several assignments for course work. I learned that professional writers talk about both the stages and process of grief work. The stages are named differently depending on the therapist you read, but generally the stages cover the process of denial, anger, bargaining, depression, and acceptance. It is a normal process that is different for different people and takes a very long time. The stages are not static nor are they clearly defined like innings in a baseball game. They spiral, and, when you think you're through one stage, you'll find yourself back there sometime in the future. For me to understand that what I was feeling was "normal grief" was both comforting and infuriating. It might have been normal, but it was *my* precious daughter and *my* personal grief.

The first stage of the grief process is *denial*. One has thoughts like "This couldn't have happened. She can't really be dead." There were moments I'd think, "Oh I want to tell her about that."

Then I would move into *anger*. I'd rage at the police investigating the accident. I was angry at God, angry at those I loved, angry at just about everything and everyone. *Bargaining* is the next stage, but I never felt I could bargain. She was dead. We had buried her.

Depression followed. This term *depression* works when I define depression as a black pit, a deep tunnel, no hope. But what I was feeling wasn't clinical depression, as I understood that medical term. It was a definable grief, an overwhelming sadness.

And the final stage is of course, *acceptance*. That has taken many, many, many years. I would at times feel I had reached it, only to find myself in an earlier "stage" triggered by a moment, a memory. This process of finding myself back in any of the stages is also a very normal response to grief. It is maddening, but normal.

Getting Started

It's critical to face these stages. If we don't do what is called "grief work" related to our losses we run the risk of being stuck in one of the stages. If we get stuck, there is a risk that the loss and the emotions of that stage begin to take over our lives. The loss can define who we are, how we think, how we see the world. It took me seven months to have the courage to begin the real therapeutic work of grieving my daughter's death. I could not bear the thought of talking about the pain, focusing on what her death meant in my life and my family's life. But the overwhelming sadness following that first Christmas nudged me into finding a therapist.

For me, the stages of anger and depression were the most difficult to work through. The first time I sat down with a therapist I cried the entire hour—and for several of the subsequent hourly meetings. I sobbed my anger at the rudeness of the police at the scene of the accident, the seeming lack of compassion from the emergency department staff and the nurses on the floor, the brusqueness of the flight attendants as we took her body for burial in another state. I had cried in the months before I saw the therapist but it was in that old controlled, "don't bother anybody" manner…that message from my childhood.

But I needed to "bother somebody" with this pain, just as you need to "bother" somebody with your pain. I needed a safe place with a therapist whom I didn't need "to take care of." I needed to be free to express my overwhelming sadness. He let me tell the story over and over. At some level I knew the people at whom I expressed my anger were doing the best they could, but it took talking about the anger with someone who didn't try to excuse it or explain it away for the intensity to begin to lift. Over the next months as I heard myself talk, as he asked exploratory questions, I could begin to have a bit of empathy about how difficult it might have been for these police, nurses, attendants to talk with me, to tell me this news, to be with me through it.

At the same time I talked about the pain and anger, I also talked about the grief and loss and the guilt and shame: the depression phase. I call it the "sadness phase." It all came out at the same time, in the same sessions as the anger. As I have said, these stages overlap; they recycle and they break through. For me, sadness at times was a sharp stabbing knife, an agonizing loneliness, an empty hole. One of the worst periods of the sadness had come before I entered therapy. Christmastime came six months after her death. Her birthday was December 22. I knew getting through that first Christmas was going to be painful, so, without really realizing it, I physically and emotionally tightened up, toughened up, and resolved to "get through it"...with a few glasses of champagne to help me out. I did not want my young sons to be denied a normal Christmas.

In looking back, I realize what a tragic mistake this was both at Christmas and in the months that followed. With my ineffective communication, tightening up, and toughing it out, I denied all of us the chance to heal as a family. Had I been able to insist on family counseling, I might have helped all of us come together in our grief. I understand part of my inability to do this was my own grief, but, with profound sadness, I know we missed an opportunity. Christmas came and went, my addiction kicked in full force, and the old patterns reemerged.

NAME

As we talked in earlier chapters about your self-image and traditional roles, I would guess you had some thoughts about the minefield of losses you had as a child or young adult. If drugs and alcohol entered our lives early we also missed many opportunities that were ultimately personal losses—loss of education, money, jobs, travel, friends, relationships, loves, connections. Identifying and reviewing those losses is a critical part of understanding what happened to you and where you might be stuck in the grief process.

The early and later losses experienced by a young girl or a woman, essentially those losses of relationships, are vital to a woman's emotional health. Parental divorce, early death of a parent, an emotionally absent mother or father, and issues of abuse all impact the self-image we have, the traditional roles we choose, our ineffective communication, and this grief we can get stuck in. In this initial stage of recovery from addiction it is helpful to *name* the losses you have had. Again some of them are simply part of normal living.

To begin to *name*, to begin to get unstuck, happens in places where we feel understanding, respect, and safety, often in work with a good counselor or therapist.

It is the role of the therapist to help us look at the patterns that keep us stuck. That can even happen initially by looking at how we connect or don't connect with the therapist. Therapists, in give-and-take relationships, must be vulnerable themselves, willing to look at the ongoing interaction in the therapy, how you as a client affect them, and how they affect you. They must be able to be with you in the feelings expressed in the therapy, in connection. They must show you that someone can be with you as you bring those frightening, shame-filled feelings into this connection.

Life Losses

A major loss creates different responses for men and women. Research indicates (and stories confirm) that men feel their greatest losses related to their work and their careers. Women feel their greatest losses in relationships. When men talk about loss, it is loss of job or loss of income or even loss of their truck. When women talk about loss it is the deep loss of meaningful connections.

For women of childbearing years, a life-changing loss can be a miscarriage, an abortion, or loss of health. During middle age, a woman who experiences a divorce or children leaving home can feel devastated. Older women often experience retirement and frequent deaths of spouses, relatives, and friends as powerful losses. Death, of course, is the ultimate and extremely lonely loss at any age whether it is loss of a parent, child, brother, sister, or friend. Perhaps the worst kind of suffering is tied up with the feeling of being rejected and left out. Loss of important, meaningful relationships is the ultimate sense of abandonment and isolation. Much of grief work begins with connecting the stories of our losses, their impact on our lives, and our responses to the losses. We often do this connecting of the meaningful stories through storytelling. Storytelling helps us begin to identify the pieces of our life's puzzle and put them together. Unless we identify the pieces and patterns, and pick them up, they simply lie on the table in front of us. Within healthy connections and through storytelling we identify the pieces of the puzzle: the corner pieces, the edges, and then the center pieces that connect by colors and shapes and patterns. We examine how they fit or relate to each other. Where does that shade of blue fit in the larger picture? And that strange shape over there? How was this loss connected with that feeling? How did that feeling relate to that behavior? How am I handling this loss now? Do I see old behavior? New choices? You also can tell your stories in journal writing, painting, drawing, or writing poetry or music, but it becomes most productive and dynamic when it moves within a connected relationship.

Nancy connected with Joe and me and started to paint. She told her story, not in a planned, organized way but by painting a feeling. She would bring the painting to therapy and talk about how she felt. The paintings were black, very dark. She began to explore the darkness, the early patterns of abuse, how she escaped to alcohol and drugs to numb the pain and the shame, and how those patterns continued in her marriage. She looked at the childhood guilt her mother inflicted on her when her mother continually told her she was responsible for her father's molestation and his ultimate abandonment of the family. She talked about her son's suicide and the guilt she felt that she had not done all she could the day before his death. She talked of her anger at the mental health professionals who minimized his symptoms. She talked about the overwhelming grief of that loss. She talked about what her son, David, meant to her. He was the one who painted and played music, the one she was connected with. She thought about and talked about how the loss, the overwhelming grief, felt at her deepest core.

She wrote letters to God:

How's David? Please tell him I love him, miss him. Sorry I didn't see it coming; he was so hurt and scared. God, we prayed for love and comfort, not to win the lottery but what the hell happened? Been mad at you. am scared to try to talk to you. Don't know anyone nuts enough to take you on. How do I get by now? you took the best in me and brok it. You gave your son willin up. I am still bitchen. I lost mine.

A mad and hart broken

Mother

In counseling, she felt it all again within relationships that were devoted to her healing. Someone once said, "To be listened to as an adult is like being held as a child."

Nancy also healed in a connected relationship with her sister, Carol. They talked about their childhood as they remembered it. Carol shared stories that validated Nancy's memories, which told Nancy she wasn't crazy for the feelings of fear and shame, for the grief she felt over a lost childhood. Talking with friends and family helps bring back memories. Listening to them gives us a way to hear their memories of what happened to them and ultimately to us. Asking others to tell us their stories begins to open our hearts and minds.

Much of the work of forming the story takes place outside of the therapy hour. The counselor asks questions and gives prompts that help you think about things in a different way and make connections among the pieces of the puzzle. You do the work as you write in your journal, take a walk, paint a picture, listen to someone else's story. You do the work as you watch what is going on in your life today—in the now. Then you return to the therapist and talk about your new thoughts, new insights, new connections. You talk about how it felt then and how it feels now.

If you are not in a place to work with a counselor, you can begin the work yourself. You retell yourself the stories. You spend time in quiet reflection. You write in a journal. You paint the pictures. You say a quiet prayer that stills the voices of judgment.

LOSS OF THE ADDICTION

The Stone Center says the most overwhelming losses for women are the losses of the chance to be in relationships that are good for us. When we are in strong, healthy relationships, we feel a sense of power and have a better sense of who we are. When an addiction is active we cannot be connected with anyone in an honest, open, truthful way. We have things to hide. We are stigmatized. We think, "If you really knew who I am you wouldn't like me." Our priorities and choices respond to the addiction, not to our personal power. In very early recovery the loss of the alcohol or drug leaves a frightening hole in our center.

For me, the alcohol filled up the hole of isolation I felt in my marriage and, as I ultimately realized, had felt my entire life. The alcohol seemed to help me let go of some of the need to control, some of the need to be the "perfect little girl." But the daily starting times came earlier and earlier, and the quantities became greater and greater. The early morning resolutions of "not today" were gone within a few hours. After those first few swallows I felt like I had joined the human race again. So how was I going to manage without this "friend" who eased my pain and helped me relax? I needed it. I deserved it!

Many of the women with whom I have worked over the years talk about this same fear. How will they manage without the hit, without the gambling, without the shopping, without the sex, without the eating, without the tobacco, without the relationship? Sorting out that sense of loss is part of the grief process we have been talking about.

As we have talked about before, first we *deny* there is a problem with comments such as "I can handle it....I'm not that bad....I don't do as much as she does....It's not affecting anybody but me." Or maybe we jump right to the bargaining phase: "I can cut down. I'll only do it on weekends." When that doesn't work either, we come face to face with the fact that this is going to be a loss of a "friend," a loss of a way to get through the day, the loss of a connection. It is a loss of something that makes us "*in*authentic" and a loss of something that "*dis*empowers" us, but a loss, nonetheless.

When we have come to the reality of the loss, when we *name* it, we often get *angry*. We get really angry at the cop who pulled us over, at the boss who confronted us, at the husband who left. "It's all their fault." Our anger usually bubbles under the surface but often breaks out in rage.

Then sometimes we *bargain*: "I'll switch to wine or beer or scotch or bourbon.... I'll lay off the hard stuff and only do marijuana.... I'll walk away from the poker machine when I've won enough for gas....I'll only go shopping once this month....I'll only see him when he's not using....I'll only smoke three cigarettes a day." But bargaining doesn't work. Addiction is cunning, baffling, and powerful.

It is at this point we often become *depressed* and sad. We miss our best friend. We get angry again. The tiger lurks in the grass. Maybe we go back to the bar or the crack neighborhood—"just to see our old friends." We go to the Christmas party without a plan. We haven't dealt with the loss, the changes we need to make, the ways to find out who we are without the "addiction friend." We haven't begun to explore ways to connect with caring, empathetic, and empowering friends, but as we begin to look at what the addiction really did to us we may have some new awareness. Would we stay with any other friend who betrayed us, ruined our relationships, and cost us our soul?

Ideally, then, the pieces of the puzzle begin to become clearer. We begin to honestly look at the losses caused by our addiction, especially the fact that we have lost *ourselves*, our self-image, our self-esteem. And we begin to realize how bad it was. I had driven the car with my children and their friends when drunk. I had gone to work drunk, been confronted, lied, and been sent home. I'd gone to parties drunk and fallen asleep at the table. Sometimes I was drunk by the time the kids came home from school. "What's wrong, Mom?" they'd ask. When I began to share these pieces of my story-puzzle with a therapist, the addiction became so very clear to me. I honestly looked at what I had lost because of this "friend." The guilt and the shame became very clear. How could I have done these things? How could I have put my children at risk, put patients and others at risk? What was wrong that I was willing to embarrass myself at parties or be shamed at work by being sent home? I was depressed, in the black pit, with no hope, no joy.

TRANSFORM

Fortunately at this time a miracle happened! I really don't know what else to call it. I was led to a book that talked about having choices in my life. The book's major premise was that, if there is something you don't like about your life, you can change it. Now these days there are thousands of self-help books that deliver that same message, but when I first heard it, I honestly was stunned. I looked up from the page, looked out the window, and saw blue sky. The book essentially said that, if I didn't like my drinking, I could change that. The book wasn't talking about drinking, but it was talking to me about my drinking. In some ways it was so simple. I had been making it so hard with my struggle about giving it up. Once I acknowledged the addiction was destroying me, destroying my relationships with my family, destroying my professional life, and leaving me empty and afraid, there really was no other choice. I had to do something, and apparently I was not able to do it all by myself.

Grief Work of Addiction

Books that encourage the general public to do grief work related to losses of divorce or retirement or even death remind us that loss does not need to be seen entirely as damaging. They encourage us to consider that growth can come out of the work. Granger Westberg says a number of hopeful things in his book *Good Grief.* He says we emerge from our grief with more maturity, more personal depth, and more faith because we've experienced the breadth and intensity of spiritual questioning and wrestling. When we wrestle with our grief, it sometimes feels as if we're in a brawl. But when we work on these issues—and sometimes it's ongoing work—we're more able to help others. We understand.

It seems to me those rewards are exactly what we need as we do the grief work of moving from addiction into recovery.

Let's examine grief work more in depth as it relates to addiction.

Denial

This is the place, in *transform,* where the reality finally breaks through the denial. Many women tell a similar story. We begin to see the pieces of the puzzle. The pieces come in different shapes and sizes. Maybe we consumed more and more of the alcohol or drugs; a family member told us of our odd behavior; we knew it ourselves at some level. A day comes when we can no longer deny the cost physically, emotionally, and spiritually.

Marla woke up in a strange bed for the second time in a month.

Barbara was confronted at work because the narcotic count was off...again.

Elaine had to be helped home from a wedding. Her sister had gone through treatment the year before and talked with her.

Two church friends came into treatment together, one right after the other. They had been sharing pills, and, when the one friend recognized the problem, the other also had courage to look at the problem.

Another client kept relapsing. Her husband owned a winery and insisted she continue to work in the gift shop. Well, guess what they sold in the gift shop and she had free access to each and every hour of each day! "If you do what you always done, you'll get what you always got."

Legal troubles such as bad checks, letting dealers use our homes as "offices," fights in bars, driving accidents, and DUIs are all behaviors that put the pieces into place. It's very difficult to deny there is a problem when we are sitting in a jail cell, or when our spouse says he is leaving if we don't stop, or when the police Breathalyzer says 0.23. We have lost control over the disease. It has us. We are addicted. Unfortunately, like all phases of the grief process, the denial creeps back in at times during even long-term recovery, but for now the reality is stronger than the denial.

For me, the grief work over both the death of my daughter and the reality of my alcoholism came together. It was that work that led me to begin my journey from broken to blessed.

Anger

The anger phase of the grief process in addiction can erupt over and over in transform or even sustained recovery—especially when issues of guilt and shame hang around. It can be triggered over a life loss such as a job loss or even a marital conflict. The feelings of anger hook right up with the loss of the addiction.

Nancy called Joe one day after several years in recovery. She was absolutely livid at her husband. Her husband had written on the calendar a note indicating the day he had decided to scatter their son's ashes. He had not asked her feelings or thoughts about this. Nancy reminded Joe of her morning ritual. Every day she touched the urn that held her son's ashes and said a meditative prayer. "It is how I start my day." This had been going on for more than ten years. She was furious at her husband for thinking he could scatter the ashes without any input from her. It was a decision that would take her son from her again. She talked with Joe again about David's death and about the guilt she felt regarding his suicide. Joe asked if her husband knew of her morning ritual. "No. I do it in private."

Later in the discussion Joe asked Nancy if she could find her voice and talk with her husband about her feelings...about not being included in the decision, about the meaning of her ritual. She didn't know. They practiced a few sentences.

Within a few days Nancy called again. She had found her voice. She had told her husband of her anger, of feeling disconnected from him and his decision, of what her ritual meant. And then she said, "We're going to take the ashes to where David used to rock climb. He loved it up there." Joe asked, "How are you with that?" After a long pause, Nancy said, "I think it's time."

It is absolutely amazing how sometimes being stuck in the anger, in the black pit, can get unstuck simply by having one's feelings heard. Of course this had been years in coming for Nancy. We can't force it or push it, but we have to do the work. We have to find the person who will listen, who will be empathetic, who helps us find the place to fit the piece. And then we take the risk to find our voice, to break the silence, to be authentic. The anger gets spoken, and when it is spoken it loses some of its control over us. Nancy had to name the anger and find a healthy way to express it before she could hear her husband's grief and his need to let go of the ashes.

The anger at the loss of the "friend" of addiction can return at any time. Just as I had to take a long look at what the loss of my role as mother and friend with my daughter meant, it was also necessary to look at what the loss of the "friend" of addiction meant. If the use of the drug/alcohol/gambling was a source of connection (even though it was inauthentic) or if it was a source of fun or helped me relax, I'd better look long and hard at how I'm now making connections, having fun, and relaxing in my recovery.

It takes immense courage to willingly "give up" an addiction. If it is all about "giving up" with little sense of what one gains from letting go of the addiction, then, I believe, recovery becomes a never-ending struggle. The depression and anger are constant battlegrounds.

Women who make it into long-term sustained recovery begin

to think about what they will gain from this new life of recovery. It is truly a feeling of hope that gives one the courage to continue through the recovery process during grief work.

Bargaining

We bargain to maintain some control of the situation. There are instances, of course, in our lives where bargaining makes some sense. In a divorce situation bargaining over money or parental visitation can be useful or destructive depending on the anger and hurt involved. However, bargaining around the disease of addiction has no positive outcome. We have no control, and bargaining gains us nothing. Once we break through the denial and acknowledge the disease, bargaining about how much or when we might be able to use again only leads us back into the disease.

I have worked with several recovering health professionals who attempted to bargain with their addiction and return to their places of work. They thought they could be around their drugs without using again. None were able to do it successfully. One nurse shifted from an intensive care unit setting to home health. Then she found her patients' home medicine cabinets calling to her addiction. A nurse anesthetist thought telling her coworkers about her addiction would keep her off the fentanyl. Sadly, no. Another nurse anesthetist moved to working in a treatment program but found that the Ativan and phenobarbital on those units called him just as strongly as the fentanyl in the operating room. A respiratory therapist working back on the hospital units after treatment found easy access to medication carts and continued his cunning addiction.

Remember, addiction is a fatal disease. I know of one recovering nurse who was found dead in the hospital stairwell. She had used 1,000 milligrams of Demerol over an eight-hour period. The pants of her uniform were covered with blood where she had injected herself through the material. Staff of the unit to which she had returned to work thought they had taken all the appropriate supportive precautions. She was not to have the narcotics keys. Other nurses working with her were asked to do the narcotic meds on her patients with her permission. But one busy evening a new nurse tossed her the narcotics keys, and the immediate compulsion of the addiction took over.

It is not unusual in a treatment program to find women who come in for treatment of alcohol, cocaine, crack, or prescription drugs who are astounded when they are told they can no longer use any mood-altering drugs of any kind—nothing. People, places, and things must change. If we go back to the bar and plan to drink just a beer or a glass of wine, it is only a matter of time before someone offers us a pill or a line or a shot. The tiger leaps out of the grass. Bargaining is not an option.

Of course, one of the reasons we bargain is because we want to hang onto whatever it is we have lost. Addiction has become an idol. We worship it as a source of our life. To heal we must be willing to give up the idol. We must acknowledge all that it has taken from us. We must make room for the new possibilities. Then we can begin to think about what will replace it.

Depression

Even when we are successful in passing through the denial, the anger, and the bargaining, we usually find ourselves in a place of depression. Again it is useful to distinguish between depression and sadness. Depression is a dark pit, hopelessness, even ugliness and stupidity. We feel that nothing can change. Sadness, on the other hand, permits a person to be more in touch with her feelings, to be more aware of the meaning of relationships and what the loss of those relationships might mean. We are aware of a deep loneliness.

When we are in the black pit of depression there is an overwhelming feeling of helplessness. "I have no choices. I am such a loser. I can't ever get out of this. I am powerless." A woman I met recently was just out of jail and waiting to go to a court- ordered ninety-day treatment program. Her husband had just told her he was leaving; her mother had to come to take care of the children. She could not stop crying. She felt helpless, powerless.

It is at this time we must remember, "Though I have no control over my addiction I am not powerless over my life or over my own decisions. I do have choices. Yes, I am powerless over other people, places, and things but not over decisions about how I relate to those people, places, and things."

One of the major steps of recovery is to begin to recognize and name those feelings of depression and sadness. Do you feel close to tears? Does your heart feel like it is breaking? We begin to know the difference between no hope (depression) and sadness. When we recognize we do have feelings and those feelings are legitimate, we begin to connect again with ourselves. We begin to realize that our feelings of sadness or grief are about the relationships we have lost. And then we realize that maybe these losses in life are related to the addiction. It is the importance of those relationships and the loss of those connections we are grieving. Once we recognize the losses as directly associated with our depression and sadness, we begin to feel more connection with ourselves. We begin to feel more authentic, more real. And we are able to value those feelings and sense some empowerment. We think, "Maybe I *can* change this. Maybe I don't ever have to feel this way about myself again." We may be led into recovery because of some negative consequence of our addiction, but we will be led out of it because of this reconnection with ourselves, with others, and with a sense of new possibilities.

Guilt and Shame

When I was most despondent and talking about my guilt surrounding the death of my daughter, well-meaning friends and even professionals told me I needed to learn to "forgive myself." I found that impossible. I went over and over and over the decisions I had made the morning of her death. I kept taking back the guilt. It was many years before I heard *forgiveness* in a more spiritual way. It made all the difference—and it changed the shape of my grief, as well as the shape of my recovery. Ultimately, it changed the shape of this book.

We have talked about guilt and shame before. They are part and parcel of grief and loss. However, guilt and shame themselves are two very separate emotions.

The guilt that comes with grief and loss is not all bad. Guilt is feeling bad for something we have done. It is about a human choice. We believe we had a choice in some situation and made the wrong decision...but it was *our* wrong decision. Guilt can be a motivating factor. After all where would we all be if we had no guilt? Guilt is something that keeps us basically on the straight and narrow. During my addiction I felt guilty about a lot of things such as speaking harshly to my children, being drunk when they came home from school, driving drunk. When my daughter died I felt terrible guilt. I would think, I should have reminded her to wear the helmet. I should have been outside with her. I should have stressed again she shouldn't cross the road. If I'd been more conscientious I could have prevented it.

Shame, on the other hand, is a loathing for who we are. Shame is toxic. It tells us we are hopelessly and permanently flawed. Shame is isolating. It seems as if we are missing a crucial part and will never get it back. It silences us. It deepens our self-doubt. Sometimes the shame comes from the old messages we heard and the chaotic circumstances in which we were raised. Sometimes this essential shame comes from the behaviors during our disease. Often it is many things together.

The sense of despair that comes with shame begins to be replaced when we start to feel the sadness. Then we begin to reconnect with ourselves. How? By telling our stories to ourselves and then to someone who can bear our feelings with us. A friend, a counselor, a pastor can help us give voice to these frightening, shameful feelings. Then they are validated. Nancy moved out of her despair and wrote about her sadness:

Just one crayon short of a full box today.
One primary color has been taken away.
God will challenge and color all that He sees,
Remember you asked me, why there's no blue leaves?

Just one crayon short of a full box, I mused
While asken the Lord, just what to do.
Too tired to trust too confused to pray
This overtaxed heart can't make another day.

Just one crayon short, by now you heard the news
There's tints, values, and there are hues.
Love is a primary color of life.
God claims and colors all that's in sight.

Just one crayon short, there's nothing more to do,
My soul's not even close to this new value.
So alone, scared, guilt on me pressed.
Could this unloved mess, come home to rest.

NANCY, POWERLESS

Unfortunately for women with addiction issues, it often takes a very long time to get to this place of finding a person, a place to share. Mental health resources are slim. Many therapists lack understanding of the disease of addiction. Many social agencies still advocate a "pick yourself up by your bootstraps" attitude.

But as we talked about with other losses, you can start with your own journaling, your own drawing, your own poetry. You begin by telling the story to yourself. You "voice" your story, and the pieces begin to fit together. You begin to understand the losses that shaped you, the loneliness you felt and still feel, and the emptiness in your soul.

SUSTAIN

Frederick Buechner is a current spiritual writer who was a Presbyterian minister. His father committed suicide when Frederick was a young boy, and he was raised in a family with the deep secrets and strict rules and roles about which we have been talking. His spiritual writings reflect his struggles with the consequences of his chaotic home and his strong relationship with God as the source of his healing.

In one of my favorite passages from his writing, Buechner says that when we are surprised to find ourselves tearing up, we should pay the tears notice because they're a message from God. That passage comes to me so very often when I find those "unexpected tears" in either myself or others. What I notice is that I often try to explain away those unexpected tears. "Well, I don't know where that came from," I say to myself, "I'm not feeling sad." One place there are unexpected tears for me is when I am talking about the material of this book, especially the forgiveness and grace of God's unconditional love. When I am talking to a group, maybe a professional group, maybe a group of recovering women, and I am talking about the clinical aspects of women's addiction, I just buzz along. But when I start to talk about my recovery and my relationship with God, sometimes my voice shakes and tears come to my eyes—summoning me "to where, if my soul is to be saved, I should go next." My recovery, my relationship with God.

Acceptance

The final stage of the process of grief resolution is acceptance. This is the place we need to "go next," but how do we get there?

One way we might get there is to expand the concept of "acceptance" into something much more active, something that isn't a final stage but that is ongoing, that evolves and grows. We reach out to something larger, grander, further connected. What do we mean by acceptance here? When we accept a gift such as a Christmas present with joy, we accept it as something we will use in an ongoing way. If it is a meaningful gift, something we have asked for or something the giver has chosen especially for us, we use it immediately. We smile. We thank the giver over and over, and we remember the giving and the acceptance as part of an evolving relationship.

Sometimes when we talk about "acceptance" as part of the final stage of the clinical grief process, we fear acceptance means the end, the letting go of the connection. I wonder if that is one reason people like myself and Nancy, people in deep grief, resist the concept or the experience of grief work. Maybe there is a fear that if we complete the grief work successfully, if we reach "acceptance," we will have erased all our feelings. We fear losing the strong sense of love and connection to that special person who is gone. In doing successful grief work of our disease of addiction we need to expand our thinking about "acceptance" into something much more than simply a void…a loss of the substance or behavior. The gift of recovery can fill that void and give us the possibility of so much more.

There is a word used in church talk that expands this new possibility in spiritual terms. The word is *metanoia,* and it means a transformation. It is more than reforming from bad behavior. It is a whole new way of thinking. Metanoia means to be transformed by the renewal of your mind. That's what needs to happen for us to integrate our recovery into a whole new way of being. I need to give up thinking about my "resolution" to quit drinking, or drugging, or eating, or bingeing, or purging, or spending, or sex. My transformed thinking frames my recovery as a gift, a new life, a new freedom.

Metanoia also leads to another church word: *repentance*. In this transformed way of thinking, we repent of our despair. We have wallowed in despair about where our lives are leading us, about who we have become. We are swamped by shame and self-loathing. We feel God has abandoned us. But when we are open to transformation, we begin to realize God has not abandoned us at all. In our addiction, our self-absorption, or in our finding an idol in our drug or behavior, we have turned our back on God. *We* have done that—not God. That is the real tragedy of addiction. We leave God. We disconnect out of our guilt and our shame. But God never leaves us. All we need to do is knock on the door and fall into God's arms full of unconditional love and forgiveness. Our loving parent is waiting there to open the door and bring us home.

New messages help us transform our ways of thinking. Well-meaning people tell us, "Forgive yourself." Buechner says that forgiving ourselves is as impossible as sitting in our own lap. We need new messages and new images. The image of "trying to sit in my own lap" makes me smile. A new image creates a new feeling.

Rather than "forgive ourselves," we need to accept God's forgiveness, God's unconditional love. When we understand and accept divine forgiveness and unconditional love we can begin to accept our human sadness that naturally comes from loss. We know the loss is part of grief. But we begin to believe in God's goodness and the fact that God has not abandoned us. We are not alone. We remember God's promise that we are already forgiven, accepted, and restored. It is not something we have to do ourselves. It has already been done. Most of the time I find that promise absolutely amazing.

Accepting the human sadness is moving into the last stage of the grief process. Again, well-meaning friends and therapists tell us we have to "let go." "Letting go" is right up there with "forgive yourself" as humanly impossible. Letting go feels like not caring anymore. Nancy couldn't let go for ten years. She needed her son near her, to be part of each day. When acceptance and letting go are "transformed" to mean understanding and accepting God's forgiveness and unconditional love, we begin to find the peace we are searching for. It's that "peace that passes all understanding."

BROKEN TO BLESSED

All of us are broken, and that's OK. It's all right because our brokenness expresses something about who we are. Our suffering and pain are much more than annoying interruptions in our lives. Rather they reach right into our uniqueness. The manner in which I am broken reveals something distinctive about me, and the way you are broken reveals something distinctive and special about you. Each person experiences suffering in a way no other person suffers. That's why when people say, "Oh, I know how you feel," you want to scream: "No, you don't!"

In *sustained* recovery, we might call this suffering a loneliness, a longing, or hunger. This longing can be thought of spiritually as a longing for home, for unconditional love, for our divine connection with God. It is part of the human condition that not just Nancy but all humans have. It is a God-shaped hole. Addictions attempt to fill that hole in our soul. It doesn't work. In recovery, we are open to God's promise that he will fill that void. We discover the joy and awe that comes from that connection.

Again, Henri Nouwen, the writer who talks about moving from

being broken to being blessed in his book *Life of the Beloved*, suggests that healing from our brokenness, our loneliness, our hunger comes from both making a friend of our addiction and placing it under the blessing. He first suggests we face this brokenness and make it our friend. When we name our brokenness in our addiction, when we name our losses and explore the grief and guilt and shame that accompany them, we no longer need to deny or run from them. He says that everything we experience, our suffering, and our pain are all part of our journey as we live out our full humanity. This is essential as we move from an "acceptance" of our disease of addiction to connecting with God, and joy fills this new life.

In my grief and fist-clenching to get through that first Christmas after my daughter's death, I was not open to receive the gift of God's grace and blessing. I was broken and closed. Only later could I risk naming my brokenness, risk a trust in God's love and forgiveness, and open my clenched fists to receive this new freedom and blessing. God healed my grief and my addiction. I ask for and receive this healing promise. Daily.

Things to *Think About*

1. What meaning do you take from your unexpected tears?
2. What do you gain by moving out of your addiction?
3. How might you make the promises of God a part of your daily life?

CHAPTER 5

M: Medical Aspects

Hi, Penny,

I hope this finds you in good health and spirits. I was thinking about you today and decided I would send these clippings about Joy. I have no clue why I cut them out to save. Maybe just a reminder...anyhow—no one (her husband) knows whether it was accidental or planned.

A recovering woman who had been in the treatment program at the same time as Joy sent me two newspaper clippings after I had moved from the area. The first clipping described her arrest for beating her husband and mother-in-law. Less than two months later, she was dead.

I had met Joy when she arrived at the outpatient program meeting intoxicated, angry, belligerent, and condescending. During her initial outpatient treatment even twenty-four hours of abstinence proved to be extremely difficult for her. She was admitted to the inpatient service after a few weeks of outpatient treatment with frequent relapses, having proved to her insurance carrier that she had "failed on an outpatient basis." Yes, Joy ultimately failed on an outpatient basis, but was it Joy who really did the failing? Or was it we therapists? A broken health care system? Given that we have recognized addiction as a physical, emotional, and spiritual disease for so many years why was it so difficult to reach Joy?

Admittedly, Joy was not easy to "care" for. Her initial angry, emotional presentation painted a true picture of her inner turmoil and pain. The irony of her name was not lost on those who tried to provide support and treatment. She was anything but joyful. Joy's multiple issues provided her a seemingly impenetrable prison in which to live most of the time. However, I also remember Joy in her brief periods of recovery when she was attending self-help, had a sponsor, completed the multiple levels of treatment, took medication for clinical depression, and genuinely sought connection with other women in recovery. But ultimately "no one knows whether it was accidental or planned." Addiction can be a fatal disease.

As we have indicated, there are many types of addictions. Alcohol, drugs, tobacco, caffeine, food, gambling, shopping, sex, and the Internet are all substances, behaviors, or compulsions that have physical and emotional aspects and consequences. Public health organizations list them as the current addictions we, the American public, are battling. All these addictions consume time, interfere with relationships, and have withdrawal symptoms. All are destructive, and some are fatal. Though some say at least half the number of people in treatment will relapse, according to *Time* magazine only about 20 percent of people who attempt to recover are able to do so (see References). As we have stated earlier, because addictions have different aspects and consequences and because each person who is addicted is unique, to be effective each woman needs individualized treatment. We will take a look at some of the approaches considered to have some validity in the professional recovering community.

Nancy now talks about another of her addictions, tobacco, and its consequences, her difficulty with breathing. "I can't even clean one of the offices without sitting down to catch my breath. I feel so exhausted. My husband has to carry in the groceries from the car." It isn't her addiction to drugs and alcohol that has caused her severe emphysema. It is her addiction to cigarettes—a pack a day for more than forty years. We often have more than one addiction at the same time. In this chapter we will talk about several kinds of addiction in which the medical aspects and consequences put the quantity and quality of our lives at real risk. They also distance us from the gift of health we have been given. *Addiction can be a fatal disease!*

Up to this point we have been talking about the emotional and spiritual issues of our lives, as women, that have contributed to our addictions—the issues that must be addressed in our recovery. In the Name portion of this chapter, we will identify the unique medical aspects and consequences for women of the various addictions. Until recently, most of the research on addictions was focused on men, but researchers were identifying particular medical aspects and consequences for women even thirty years ago. We will describe why addiction must be considered a chronic disease. We will compare it with other chronic diseases, such as diabetes and heart disease, which have less social stigma but similar attributes and prognosis.

We will also look at the reality of "co-occurring diseases." The term *co-occurring* means there is an addiction existing at the same time as a mental illness. This coexisting phenomenon exists in a large percentage of women with addictions and must be a major part of each woman's assessment and treatment.

In addition to *naming* the medical aspects of various drugs and various addictions we will briefly look at the social consequences of women's addictions.

In the Transform section we will talk about actions we might take to minimize the medical consequences of addictions including some hallmarks of effective treatment programs. Some of the newer strategies used in treatment programs will be briefly described.

We will also look at the actions that empower us to take responsibility for our own health. Substance addictions in particular affect every organ in the body, so a holistic approach to our health is necessary.

The Sustain section will stretch our concept of healing to consider the holistic component of spiritual aspects of addiction. Focus on spiritual healing and restoration includes thoughts of holding ourselves and our addictions within God's loving grace. Being held by God suggests having a sense of being blessed, a sense of belonging to God, and a sense of hope and joy.

NAME

When one is able to finally come to grips with the reality that one has a disease and it is the disease of addiction, one can begin to develop ideas and strategies to specifically combat the disease. If I think I have a bad cold but it turns out to be a sinus infection, there is a whole different way I get well. If I think I have strained a muscle in my leg, but it turns out to be a fracture, I need different help. If I think I have a slight drinking problem or a little problem with cocaine, but it turns out to be an addiction, there are other ways I can heal.

In the following section you will find a considerable number of medical terms, research findings, and statistics regarding the aspects and consequences of the disease of addiction. Though one can sometimes "glaze over" when reading medical terms and numbers, this information is critical to understanding the individual and communal risks of this disease.

Addiction is a definable disease listed in the *Diagnostic and Statistical Manual of Mental Disorders (DSM-IV)* of the American Psychiatric Association. A recent television special coproduced by the National Institutes of Health and Home Box Office (HBO 2007) entitled *Addiction* specifically states that addiction is a brain disorder in which the brain's neurologic pathways are changed by the drug used. The changes can be long lasting even after the drug use has stopped. However, the good news is that some of the neurologic changes are reversible after prolonged abstinence.

As noted earlier, addiction has similarities to other diseases. And just like other diseases, addictions have specific symptoms, but these symptoms are often not precise and develop over a long period of time.

A very important aspect of the disease of addiction is accepting that this *is* a *chronic* disease. A chronic disease is one of a "long duration." Though some people respond to the first treatment and never have another occurrence, the more usual response in addiction is unpredictable relapse.

Additionally, it is vital for women to consider the potential damage done to every organ through addictive use of substances.

A Chronic Disease

To understand the chronic nature of addiction, it is helpful to compare addiction with other chronic diseases such as diabetes or heart disease. That comparison between diabetes and addiction is apt, as both diseases begin with a long period of mild symptoms before an "official" diagnosis. In diabetes, as in addiction, treatment approaches need to be individualized, and recovery periods sometimes are effective and oftentimes need frequent adjustment.

For me, the stark reality of the chronic nature of addiction compares directly with that of my chronic heart disease. A few years ago, after ignoring squeezing sensations in my arms when exercising, I learned I had 95 percent blockage in the main artery of my heart. During the months I was experiencing the symptoms, I told myself, "This can't be a heart problem. The pain is in my arm, not in my chest. My family dies of strokes, not of heart attacks." (Denial, minimization.) In my family, there is a genetic component for strokes (just like the genetic component for my alcoholism), and I had been taking blood pressure medication for years. I'm a nurse. I should have made the connection of my symptoms to my genetic predisposition.

My physician first treated my clogged artery by implanting a stent—a small wire inserted in the clogged artery to open it. This was a new treatment at the time and not too invasive. I did all the suggested lifestyle adjustments including increased exercise, decreased cholesterol intake, and new medication. It didn't work. I had renewed symptoms after several months (scarring around the stent and more plugged arteries). This time I paid attention, and we tried new strategies. Just as in addiction, sometimes the first treatments such as attending self-help, outpatient, or day treatment don't work either, even when you feel like you are doing all the right things. Finally after continued recurrent symptoms, one year later other arteries were continuing to clog, and I had cardiac bypass surgery.

Now after six years, I am doing fine but I must be aware of the required changes in my lifestyle every day. That's the chronic nature of heart disease. If I don't reduce my fat intake, exercise vigorously, and take my medications faithfully, I will be back in the hospital for more major surgery. Some statistics say 50 percent of people who have bypass surgery have to have it redone within five years. This feels so much like my chronic disease of alcoholism; if I don't pay attention to what I need to do every day, I will be back into the acute phase of the disease of alcoholism.

UNIQUE CONSEQUENCES OF ADDICTION FOR WOMEN

Alcohol

One of the things I have learned about women and heart disease is that we often delay getting treatment for our symptoms. We minimize the severity of the chest pain or the arm pain or the shortness of breath. Why do we do that? Perhaps because we "don't want to bother anyone," and we don't want the stigma of being sick. We are the caretakers. We sometimes minimize our symptoms of the disease of addiction for the same reason.

In many instances the clinical symptoms of addiction and the consequences for women remain much the same as they were thirty years ago. Of course there are some differences because of such things as new drugs, earlier ages of beginning use of drugs, the popularity of binge drinking, and the increase in associated risky sexual behavior. However, many of the currently identified aspects and consequences are the same ones we heard about decades ago. Much of the following information is from recent studies from Columbia University (CASA; see References):

- It appears we still continue to consume lesser amounts of substances but get into physical difficulties earlier. This phenomenon is called "telescoping" and is apparent for women in the damage done to the brain, the liver, and the heart.
- In the brain, the consequences are age related. For an adolescent the toxic effects of alcohol or drugs during a critical time of brain development cause more damage to mental capacity than heavy drinking as an adult. An older woman who drinks more than one drink a day is at risk for premature aging, mental confusion, irritability, short-term memory loss, and difficulty in problem solving.
- Cirrhosis of the liver and other liver diseases develop in women sooner and at lower levels of drinking than in men who drink. Pancreatitis, an inflammation of the organ that regulates insulin, is an outcome of heavy drinking, hence one reason for the association of alcoholism and diabetes.
- Heart disease is the number one killer of women, and alcohol/ drug abuse can be a contributing factor to heart attacks, irregu-

lar heart rate, and disease of the heart muscle. Severe bleeding (hemorrhaging) in blood vessels throughout the body can lead to death. A bleeding ulcer can cause severe pain and ultimately death. "Bleeding out" in her apartment hallway because of severe alcoholism was the recent cause of death of a talented friend and vivacious woman writer and therapist in Chicago. This woman had truly struggled with alcoholism and other addictive drugs for years. She had been hospitalized numerous times for pancreatitis and internal bleeding. She knew if she drank again she would probably die. Addiction *can be* a fatal disease.

- It also appears even women who are moderate drinkers have an increased risk of breast cancer. One study found that women who drink approximately three drinks a day have a one-third greater risk for development of breast cancer than women who do not drink. There seems to be a link between alcohol and estrogen that may cause this interaction.

Other drugs

Prescription drugs, over-the-counter drugs, and illegal drugs all have severe withdrawal and long-term consequences.

Painkillers, tranquilizers, and sedatives place the user at risk for effects such as sudden respiratory depression. Sudden withdrawal from these drugs can lead to symptoms such as diarrhea, vomiting, and seizures. Think of all the names of celebrities who have recently died or overdosed and their symptoms.

Stimulants and steroids can lead to mood swings, irritability, and even violence.

Amphetamines and cocaine each have their own consequences in withdrawal such as depressed mood, bad dreams, insomnia or excessive sleep, fatigue, and increased appetite. Cocaine use can cause coke-triggered strokes and heart attacks from sudden elevated blood pressure and constriction of blood vessels.

Heroin is seen as the most lethal of the illicit drugs and either kills many of its users or keeps them hooked for the rest of their lives. Severe medical consequences of high blood pressure, liver and pulmonary diseases, and HIV/AIDS are common.

Over-the-counter drugs are frequently used by teenagers and cause their own set of problematic consequences. Diet pills, as well as diuretics, emetics, and laxatives, are used by women with eating disorders to lose weight. Over-the-counter cold medicines contain as much as 40 percent alcohol and are drugs of abuse. Tobacco is an over-the-counter drug!

Polysubstance abuse, which means the use of several classes of drugs at the same time, is frequent among drug users. One study found that 44 percent of college polysubstance users (binge drinking and using drugs) are women. One large study found that more than half of deaths caused by accidental overdose can be attributed to using two or more drugs in combination.

Methamphetamine

Methamphetamine is considered by some professionals in the field of addiction as the most dangerous drug on the market. Because it is inexpensive and fairly simple to make, the epidemic has taken over many rural communities. "Shoppers" gather the chemical ingredients, and "cookers" concoct their toxic brew in home laboratories prone to fires.

Meth users say it puts you on top of the world. But as it wears off you feel helpless and depressed; terrifying hallucinations are common. Users sometimes go on binges and stay up for days. Premature aging, body sores, and teeth disfigurement result from heavy use. Long-term risks include brain damage, stroke, liver damage, extreme weight loss, and exposure to HIV and AIDS.

Seven out of ten women who use meth have a history of physical and sexual abuse. Some start out thinking they'll lose weight by using meth, and, before they know it, addictive behaviors land them in prison, treatment, or the hospital. It is *very difficult* to get into the recovery process from meth, but, as Moms Off Meth (www.momsoffmeth.com), a self-help group started in Iowa, shows, there is always hope. With the support of self-help groups and frequent contact with women mentors, these women are maintaining recovery. Connection with support groups and with their children gives them an environment with choices and support.

Other Addictions

Tobacco

We all know smoking is an addiction and can be fatal. There are some specific statistics worth mentioning (*Time;* see References):

- Each year approximately 178,000 women die of a smoking-related disease.
- More women die each year in the United States of lung cancer than of breast, uterine, and ovarian cancers *combined.*
- Approximately 3,000 children and teens become regular tobacco users *each day;* almost half of them are girls.
- There are many, many other alarming general statistics related to the use of tobacco and its disease consequences, but, since our discussion is focused on women, we will concentrate on the impact of tobacco use and women.

As Nancy's earlier message tells us, smoking also causes debilitating respiratory diseases such as bronchitis, emphysema, and chronic obstructive pulmonary disease. Smoking increases the risk of death of these diseases. It is responsible for 90 percent of the respiratory-related deaths in women. In older women smoking is linked to decreased ability to live independently because of weakened muscles. Also, smoking causes macular degeneration, which is the leading cause of blindness in elderly Americans. The risk of fractures is more than double among older women smokers. Between the ages of sixty-five and seventy-four years, women who smoke are more than twice as likely to die as women who don't smoke.

Other dysfunctions and dark places

Earlier in this book I indicated that the things we talk about here might be useful to women who do not have a specific alcohol or drug addiction but possibly struggle with eating disorders, sexual addictions or dysfunctions, gambling problems, or a whole array of shadowed places. These issues, too, have medical aspects and consequences.

Consider the issues of eating disorders. Most of us know about the direct consequences of severe eating disorders, consequences of unbalanced electrolytes, cardiac irregularities, and even death. Often teenaged girls who engage in unhealthy dieting also engage in significant alcohol abuse. Bulimic women who are also alcohol dependent have higher rates of other substance abuse, suicide attempts, and other mental health disorders.

Sexual addictions, sexual dysfunctions, and even risky sexual activity are often associated with alcohol and drug use. Unprotected sex is one of the primary concerns for women who use drugs and alcohol. Medical consequences for unsafe sex include sexually transmitted diseases (STDs) and the AIDS virus. Two-thirds of AIDS cases in American women are associated with drug abuse. Often the sex that transmits the AIDS virus is with a man who injects drugs.

Female adolescents have alarming incidences of STDs. A 2008 report from the Centers for Disease Control and Prevention gives significant statistics for teenaged girls infected with at least one sexually transmitted infection (STI). The relationship between STIs and drug use is clear. Teens who have used drugs are five times more likely to have unprotected sex than those who do not use drugs. One study found that teenaged girls who used marijuana at least three times in the last month were twice as likely to be sexually active as, and 25 percent less likely to use sexual protection than, those who had never used marijuana.

Food, shopping, gambling, and Internet compulsions are disorders that are not always considered addictions but that qualify as behaviors that disrupt normal relationships. Fifteen percent of mildly obese people are compulsive eaters, and there appears to be a link between food addiction and depression. Gambling and Internet compulsions are thought to be impulse-control problems that affect relationships similarly to substance abuse addictions.

Co-occurring disorders

As mentioned earlier, many people who are addicted to drugs or alcohol also experience mental health problems at some point in their lives. For a woman to have a reasonable chance to recover from her addiction and stabilize her mental health problem, the mental health disorder and the addiction must be treated at the same time.

How do co-occurring diseases develop? The co-occurrence process can start before or after the use of drugs or alcohol. Sometimes *before* drug use becomes an addiction, persons with mental health problems use drugs to self-medicate the unpleasant symptoms of the mental illness. For example, a person with an anxiety disorder might use alcohol to quiet her "nerves." A person with depression might find an amphetamine gives her the energy she needs to get on with her day.

With other persons the mental illness develops *after* the person starts using the drugs or alcohol. A teenager is doing OK; she starts using a lot of marijuana and then hallucinogens. Some intrusive thoughts or voices start occurring more frequently, even when she isn't using drugs. This might indicate the person was vulnerable to the mental illness before the start of the drug use. In other words, she might have a genetic risk of a mental illness that has not manifested itself until she ingests a mood-altering drug; or she might be a victim of sexual abuse and the drug use increases the symptoms of the posttraumatic stress disorder.

Illnesses that frequently co-occur with addiction include

- Anxiety disorder
- Attention-deficit hyperactivity disorder
- Bipolar disorder
- Conduct disorder
- Depression
- Posttraumatic stress disorder
- Schizophrenia

The links among depression, suicide, and substance abuse are predominant in all age categories for women and across all economic classes. Teenaged girls, adult women, and mature women who are substance abusers are very likely to suffer bouts of depression. Suicidal thoughts and attempts are almost double those of women who do not abuse substances.

It is vital that all providers in treatment programs evaluate mental health issues as part of any addiction treatment assessment. The implications for finding a treatment program that screens and treats co-occurring diseases are critical.

I'm not certain how we could have "cared for" Joy differently. She had ongoing mental health evaluations with intervention (antidepressants). She was in a program with a gender-specific focus, and spiritual topics were frequently discussed. She remained empty and angry. It seems Joy never filled her spiritual emptiness, and the result proved fatal.

Pregnancy

The problems that arise with pregnancy and substance abuse are well documented. There have been hundreds of public health and prevention campaigns that address the problems, but many women continue to minimize the potentially devastating effects of even light to moderate use of tobacco, alcohol, or illicit drugs. Smoking, drinking, or use of drugs places the pregnancy and developing baby at risk for miscarriage, stillbirth, premature birth, low birth weight, or congenital defects. The baby's brain can so easily be affected, resulting in mental retardation, poor cognitive skills such as problem solving and arithmetic, and behavioral disorders. These problems can continue as the child develops through adolescence and adulthood. Sometimes the child's problems are as serious as or worse than those of the mother.

Almost every woman wants to have a healthy baby, so pregnancy would seem to be a high motivator for helping women to stop smoking, drinking, or using drugs. Unfortunately almost 50 percent of pregnancies are unplanned. In fact 80 percent of teen pregnancies are unplanned, and 55 percent of those occur when the teenager is under the influence of drugs and alcohol. Sixty percent of women who drink do not know they are pregnant until after the first trimester. Pregnancy adds stress to most women's lives, and increasing smoking and drinking is a common coping mechanism. Women who are depressed and/or victims of partner violence increase substance abuse during pregnancy. This leads to greater risk for major depression, miscarriage, and premature labor.

Smoking tobacco and marijuana increases the carbon monoxide levels and reduces levels of oxygen to the fetus. This can lead to miscarriage, sudden infant death syndrome, bronchitis, asthma, and pneumonia. Newborns of smoking mothers often have low birth weight, chronic ear infections, and tonsillitis. Cleft palate and cleft lip are more common in babies whose mothers smoked. A pregnant woman who uses drugs, alcohol, tobacco, and so forth has the double stigma of damaging her own body and that of her unborn baby. Sadly, she may believe she has few options to interrupt her addiction. Perhaps she has other children to care for, which cuts down her options for treatment. She may have no health insurance. She may fear legal intervention for her drug use. For various reasons, women who use drugs are less likely to obtain good prenatal care.

Social consequences

Though it is beyond the scope of this discussion to talk in any depth of the consequences to society of women's substance abuse, there are several topics important to the broader picture.

Rape, violence, and prostitution are tragic aspects of women's drug addiction. A woman who has been raped or assaulted may use drugs to cope with the physical and emotional pain from the assault, or because of her drug addiction a woman places herself at higher risk for rape and assault.

Prostitution is both a cause and a consequence of drug addiction. Women often sell themselves to pay for drugs. Unfortunately, prostitutes are unlikely to require use of condoms, making them highly vulnerable to STDs.

Women who break drug laws and commit drug-related crimes are the fastest-growing portion of the prison population. There was a 27 percent increase of women arrested for drunk driving between 2002 and 2007! The total number of women in prison, many of whom have children, increased enormously in the 1980s and 1990s, mostly because of drug-related crimes. Many of these women are victims of abuse and battering, have economic problems, and are single parents, which then means they are at high risk of having their children placed in custodial care.

The crack epidemic is part of the reason for the explosion in female prison populations. The effects of crack are short-lived and push a woman into criminal acts to buy another hit. Robbery, burglary, and drug dealing are some of the more violent crimes associated with the crack epidemic. Shoplifting, pickpocketing, selling stolen goods, and forging checks are often done to get drugs.

Few prisons have any sort of drug treatment programs. Drug offenders who do not receive treatment in prison or outside on their release are at high risk of relapse into drug use, and seven out of ten will return to prison. Something *must* change.

TRANSFORM

Given all the medical consequences of addiction, there is clearly a need for a comprehensive change in lifestyle for a recovering woman. If the addiction has affected every organ of her body, then every organ of her body needs repair. In this discussion of *transforming* our lives, we will first discuss some ideas regarding treatment and what to look for in a treatment program, as well as some things one might expect from a counselor. Also we will think about the "double whammy" of co-occurring mental health problems and what that term means as one moves along in recovery. And we will talk about the empowerment of women as they assume responsibility for changes in their own lifestyles.

Treatment

The depth and breadth of treatment programs have changed and been modified significantly over the past seventy years. From "drying-out" units, to self-help, to thirty-day inpatient programs, to outpatient programs and aftercare, many tactics have been attempted in an effort to find what gives the best opportunity for successful recovery.

The more recent approaches to treatment, thirty-day inpatient treatment programs, were popular from about 1965 to 1995. Generally, those programs disappeared when insurance refused to pay, although some self-pay programs continue to make something more than detox an option. Some state programs have services that last into a month or even several months. Most of those programs include several levels of care including residential-type housing. And sometimes there are programs that allow women to bring their children. Though professionals in the field often rail at the loss of longer treatment, in all honesty, we must acknowledge that thirty-day treatment programs were very expensive and not terribly successful. Success rates generally ran about 20 to 50 percent even with the longer programs. One can hardly fault insurance companies for refusing to pay for what didn't work. After all, would you continue to buy a brand of car that started less than half the time?

So if you are considering entering recovery at any level from self-help to inpatient treatment in hopes of giving your recovery the best possible chance of success, what should you be looking for? There are some benchmarks that are considered indicators of quality service.

Program Qualities to Look for

One hallmark of a successful program philosophy is that it encourages a person to enroll before she reaches "rock bottom." There is an old myth that a person has to reach "bottom" before she can be helped. That is not true. In fact, if someone still has her job and family she has a much better chance of recovery than someone who has lost everything. She has support. Fortunately, the attitude of self-help and health professionals has changed over the years. So, if you are a woman who has received the gift of recognizing the addiction early, of seeing the early signs of what you stand to lose, please remember that the earlier the disease is treated, the better the chance of your success.

Also, look for a program that uses a combination of approaches and is individualized for the particular problems each woman faces. Effective programs often use a cognitive-behavioral approach that encourages the client to explore the relationship between her thinking and her actions. Look for the following:

- Motivational interviewing explores your choices and options (empowerment).
- Contingency management will ask you: "What will happen if you lose your job? What will happen if you have to go to jail?"
- Twelve-step attendance means an involvement with Alcoholics Anonymous or Narcotics Anonymous. These self-help organizations have helped many people for more than seventy years. But not everyone finds it the "only" approach to recovery. If available, "women's only" meetings can be a safe place to begin.
- Family therapy focuses on the effects of addiction on every member, and it's not about blaming or attacking the person with the disease.
- Women's addiction is unique, and women's recovery is unique, so a gender-specific approach is highly recommended.
- The issue of co-occurring mental health problems is so critical to recovery that it is highly recommended that a treatment program have a credentialed psychiatrist on the treatment staff.
- A spiritual component helps begin an awareness of the divine presence.
- Attendance at long-term aftercare, phone calls, and alumni reunions can all be part of helping the recovering woman maintain her recovery.

Newer Strategies: Harm Reduction and Methadone Maintenance

Many therapists and recovering persons continue to believe that total abstinence is the only valid approach to recovery. Others seek to reduce the harm. Harm reduction operates along a continuum from "safer use" to "managed use" to "abstinence." It is an attempt to meet users "where they are" rather have a "one size fits all" approach to treatment. This approach does not minimize the tragic harm and danger associated with drug use but recognizes people's vulnerability and capacity to deal with drug-related consequences. Although abstinence is always the goal, this approach recognizes that no matter how far the disease has progressed the person's basic human core remains. And it seeks the treatment of drug addiction rather than incarceration in the penal system. But it's not without its risks. Fatal accidents can still occur.

Methadone maintenance is another approach to reducing the harm of drug use. It is used in the treatment of heroin addiction and is primarily a replacement therapy. When heroin is used, it releases an excess of a neurotransmitter, dopamine, in the brain. This excess release causes the user to need a replacement opiate continuously to fill in this receptor site in the brain. Methadone, a substitute drug, which is distributed under closely controlled legal and medical conditions, can fill in this receptor site. This replacement permits the addict on methadone to change his or her behavior and stop heroin use. Methadone reduces the cravings for heroin and blocks the highs from heroin. Ultimately the client does not experience the uncontrolled, compulsive, and disruptive behavior seen in heroin addicts. Decreased illegal behaviors is a positive outcome for persons enrolled in a methadone program.

Relapse

In addiction, just as with any chronic disease, relapse, recurrence, exacerbation are a common, painful occurrence. Return to drug use after a period of being drug free can be caused by many things. Sometimes these happen together, and sometimes a single issue can lead to relapse. Common red flags can be

- Drug-related sights, sounds, smells, thoughts, or dreams connected to the drug of choice can trigger a craving or drug seeking:
- A movie showing snorting or injecting
- Return to people, places, things where you used
- Stress or a negative mood:
- A fight with your kids, a breakup with your boyfriend, work-related tension
- Positive mood or celebrations:
- A wedding, a new job
- A taste of the drug itself, even in a small amount:
- A "nonalcoholic" beer

Once a trigger is initiated it is often very difficult to overcome the craving. Even though there have been devastating consequences in the past or future disastrous effects are clear, the person feels overwhelmed by the desire to use. The desire to use can begin before a person is even aware of it. The desire to "reward" oneself has a head start on clear decision making. Some people have more trouble managing these powerful brain-chemical impulses than others.

Strengthening Recovery

Any treatment opportunity offers a decided advantage. We have a chance to explore our unique issues as individuals and, as women, get some insights into this disease, how it developed in our lives, and where we might go from here. We can work with other women who understand our issues and needs. And if we're lucky, we'll find others with whom we can explore our own spiritual core.

Whether you are just beginning to address these addiction issues, whether you are in structured treatment, or whether you are moving along in the recovery process more independently, there are a number of things you can take responsibility for that will help stabilize these medical aspects and consequences. And remember, because the disease has affected all of our organs, we need to take a very holistic approach to our recovery.

Get Medical and Dental Examinations

One of the easiest and first efforts you can make in your recovery is to have a thorough physical and dental exam. In the midst of addiction we are likely to have ignored, denied, and minimized the effects of the drugs, and we have ignored our general health. Early detection of any significant consequences can protect us from further problems and the stress of serious medical problems. A thorough physical exam, with our honest answers to questions about drug and alcohol use, will include blood work, chest x-ray films, and a Pap smear. Blood work will identify things such as high cholesterol, diabetes, infection, and anemia. A chest x-ray exam will look at the effects of smoking and signs of tuberculosis. A Pap smear will identify any signs of uterine or cervical cancer. Also the assessment of our heart, lungs, abdomen, and circulation will identify problems such as high blood pressure, tenderness in organs, and artery or vein damage.

In addition to the direct consequences of addiction on our bodies, many of us ignored general prevention strategies such as mammograms and updated immunizations. If these health strategies are not part of your health insurance, there are many public health clinics and foundations that provide low-cost or financially supported avenues to have these issues addressed. Women you may meet in self-help and counselors could help you find these supports in your community. Phone calls to public health clinics, hospitals, and community mental health clinics provide resources. If you are a teenager or college student a school health center counselor can be a great resource. Senior women can find many resources through services for the aging. Clergy are also aware of many resources through the church and community. It may take some investigation on your part, but it is part of your new responsibility to yourself and to your recovery. Doing all this means you care for yourself in a new way. Following are some additional things you can focus on to assist your recovery.

Manage Your Stress

Stress can trigger anxiety that often leads to relapse. Now that addiction is conceptualized as a brain disorder, the link between stress and addiction is becoming even clearer. A stressful occurrence or situation increases the craving for the drug or alcohol. When you are under stress at work, when you have too many activities on the calendar, when there is conflict in your relationships at home, you feel under stress, and a hit, a shot, a pill, a smoke sounds good. We think, after all, the drug has worked in the past. An increased awareness of the stress and some new coping strategies are critical to recovery. Review the techniques of body awareness, releasing the tension, physical exercise, and meditation as stress releasers we talked about in Chapter 2. Look at your calendar and your scheduler. Are there so many activities and appointments there is hardly any white space empty? What can you say no to? "No" is a complete sentence! What can you identify as a priority, and what can wait? Where can you ask for help from a friend, a sister, your mother, your significant other so you can get to a meeting? Articles on stress management in women's magazines give other suggestions.

Stress and anxiety are compounded when we have a co-occurring disorder. Depression, anxiety disorder, and posttraumatic stress disorder can place women's recovery in real jeopardy. Continued mental health assessment with appropriate use of medication can make success in recovery a likely possibility. Particularly if a woman has successive relapses, the issue of stress in her life and her coping strategies for dealing with it are of critical importance.

You are the expert on your body and on your stress reduction and, therefore, the expert on your recovery!

Make Nutrition a Priority

Today's nutritionists tell us we all crave sugar, salt, and fat. And we indulge in them. That's why we're an obese nation. Another recovery term, "HALT," means don't let yourself get too *H*ungry, *A*ngry, *L*onely, or *T*ired. This term certainly addresses the stress and nutrition components of holistic recovery and may help us remember to eat wisely. Besides drinking plenty of water and eating our fruits and vegetables, another basic approach to good nutrition is to read food labels to have a better chance of eating a diet low in fat and salt. Here are some things to look for if you are considering a 2,000-calorie-a-day diet:

- Fat—Choose foods that have zero trans fats and are low in saturated fats.
- Carbohydrates—These days low-carb diets are popular, but carbohydrates are essential for energy. Work on keeping carbs to 130 grams per day.
- Whole grains—Eat about 3 ounces per day. Some chips and cookies are now made with whole grains, but read the labels.
- Sodium or salt—Keep intake below 2,300 milligrams daily.

To eat fewer prepared foods, try your hand at cooking creatively. There are some terrific television shows that demonstrate not only basics in cooking but also delicious gourmet recipes. You can find cookbooks by the thousands from beginners to gourmet chefs—many in your local library. Buy a Crock-Pot, and use the low-fat recipes. It helps you create a healthy meal that is essentially ready when you arrive home from work or the kids' activities. A wonderful activity is to start grocery shopping and cooking with your kids. Start with recipes they will enjoy cooking and eating.

And cut down on serving sizes. The biggest cause of our weight gain is not what we eat but the size of the servings. If we could just cut down on the junk snacking and the portions at meals, we wouldn't need fancy and expensive diets. Four small meals a day is better than three large meals. It keeps our sugar levels at a more even balance. A cup of hot chocolate made with fat-free milk about 4 PM (maybe even with two marshmallows!) is a nice treat. When I make it with low-fat milk and even some leftover coffee from the morning, it becomes an inexpensive latte.

Find Time to Exercise

Ten minutes a day can make a difference. First get an OK from your primary care professional when you get that physical exam, and then get a decent pair of walking shoes, take a deep breath, and walk for ten minutes to start. Recent reports say that amount of exercise can reduce your risk of major disease and greatly improve your quality of life. Sometimes we don't start any exercise because we think it has to be intense and long. But just getting started will make a difference in your health and how you feel. As recovery becomes a new way of living, there will be added incentive, motivation, and pleasure in increasing the time and concentration of your exercise. Read magazines in your library about exercise ideas.

It would be great to join a gym, but that costs money. How about a yoga class at the local YWCA? Our local rec department has a belly-dancing class. Doesn't that sound fun? How about taking the kids for a walk after dinner? It's a wonderful time to get them to talk and for you to listen.

SUSTAIN

This focus on the medical aspects of addiction and the physical consequences is essential to our recovery, but, even if addiction is a physiologic brain disorder with costs to every part of our physical body, there is also a core spiritual component to this disease. Focus on and attention to this foundational spiritual component is crucial for holistic healing. Exploring the spiritual aspects of the disease and recovery begins early, when we are first wondering if maybe we have a problem here. For many of us that time tells us something is painfully diseased at our spiritual core. In this stage of *sustain*, we will define essential healing as the restoration of our souls, as well as our bodies.

When we are consumed by the addiction, we become fearful and hopeless. Over and over we try to stop. We think we are failures. The sense of failure leads to further anxiety, fear, and despair. We have broken homes, broken careers, broken relationships, and broken selves.

Finally our broken self says, "My God, help me!" When I finally unclenched my fists and deeply prayed those words, I began to feel a slight movement, a gleam of hope. Just as our physical and emotional health allows us to be open to the adventure of daily life, our spiritual health opens us to an adventure of hope and joy. When we are fully alive, fear and despair shift into a new openness. It can happen in the blink of an eye, but it's often a slow process to fully move from broken to blessed. When the opening does come, this overwhelming sense of hope leads us to whole new ways of thinking and feeling and being.

FROM BROKEN TO BLESSED

To be human is to be broken. When we are broken we forget what fills that God-shaped empty space each of us has. The emptiness in our broken selves is the core of the human qualities of our longings, our anxieties, and our fears. You and I have attempted to fill that void with our addictions and behaviors. As a result, we have caused ourselves and those we love unhappiness, pain, and tragedy. Our fears and anxieties penetrated our self-image. Our relationships broke. Those broken relationships led to further feelings of rejection and abandonment. Addiction itself is at the root of our brokenness, but the spiritual consequence is in our sense of despair and hopelessness.

Often, we pray to be healed and then feel abandoned when the struggle continues. We think, if God really loved us, he would take this all away. Theologians have wrestled with that concept for thousands and thousands of years. It is the theme of many books of the Bible and thousands of essays, sermons, and studies. I certainly do not have the answer, but one thing that has helped me move out of the struggle is changing the language of my prayers.

As I have said earlier, while still in my active addiction I would walk around the house at night asking, "My God, what am I going to *do* about this?" Slowly, very slowly, probably over the years rather than over those first weeks or months, I heard my prayer changing to "My God, how am I to *be* in this? How am I to *be* with myself? How am I to *be* with others, and most important how am I to *be* with you?" By changing our language, we expand our awareness. We become aware that the things we need to "do" are things for our physical and emotional recovery, *and,* in addition to doing, there is a crucial core of finding our authentic and open and honest connections with ourselves, with our loved ones, and with God. This crucial core is the courage and creativity of "being" our new authentic selves in *sustained* recovery.

For me this crucial core included an acceptance that it is not about "what I am going to do about this," but rather, "Can I be open to a way of being with this disease that helps me embrace it, to use it to learn about myself and others, and to learn about your presence in my life?"

Accepting and embracing this disease is a slow process. Slowly, very slowly I have been able to change the word for this journey from "struggle" to "challenge." Think about the difference between those two words. If you picked up a travel magazine and found an article about a hiking vacation that was described as "a struggle," would you go? No! But if it said "challenging," you might. A challenge describes something I might willingly accept and even welcome. The challenge of this disease of addiction brings a slight smile to my lips. Yeah, I can take this on, with God's promise.

Of course we have so many other life challenges as well and so many things twittering and tweeting for our attention. But accepting this challenge of recovery requires an ever-present awareness and consciousness of its number one priority.

Let's look at another example of a challenge. Say you didn't finish high school. Now you're ready to take on the GED challenge, or maybe you feel it's time to enter college. If you think your future depends on obtaining that degree, you will do a lot of things to make that happen. You might visit a counselor to determine what courses to take. You might read, study, write, take examinations, make hard choices about how to spend your money, carve out time and space. You think, "It's all worth it. My future depends on this."

Well, your future, in fact your very life, depends on your acceptance of the challenge of recovery. The spiritual core of your recovery depends on doing whatever it takes to keep this blessed recovery challenge as your number one priority. How do you do that?

A New Openness

You go back to those effective communication skills—you listen.

You read—maybe Anne Lamott, maybe Henri Nouwen, maybe Frederick Buechner, maybe Barbara Brown Taylor, maybe the Psalms, maybe poetry, maybe something you know you have loved in the past (see Resources)

You write—maybe a journal, maybe poetry, maybe a story about where you are now and what is important to you.

You listen to sacred music.

You examine yourself in the morning and at night about an awareness of God's presence today. You look for the miracles of that day.

You find quiet time to mediate, a place to embrace your spiritual center.

And you pray.

As a child, I was taught that prayer required my assuming a position of focused attention and piety. What I have come to believe as an adult is any increased awareness of and attention to my relationship with God is prayer. What a relief!

"Whose" You Are

Kathleen Norris (see Resources) has written many books about her spiritual journey. She says prayer isn't asking for what you think you want, but it's asking to be changed in ways you can't even begin to imagine. Change is not having *to prove* I am God's precious daughter but *to believe* the truth of that promise. Put simply, life is a God-given opportunity to become who we are, to affirm our own true spiritual nature, to claim our truth, to believe and incorporate God's promise into the reality of our being...to "be."

Bookstores are full of books telling you how to "find the real you." This one, in fact, has spent some time exploring the questions "Who am I?" and "Why am I that way?" But the question that moves us from broken to blessed is "Whose am I?" And the answer is that you are God's daughter. No matter how much pain you have caused, you are loved, and you belong to God. Isn't that the message we long to hear? Isn't that the message that quiets the despair and hopelessness? Isn't that the message that fills our "God-shaped emptiness"? I am always so greatly reassured when I read "Nothing can separate you from my love for you." Every time I screw things up, I pray to remember this.

Remember those statistics that say only about two women out of ten move into long-term recovery? How can we be one of those two? How can we ever do this alone? We *must* stake our lives on the message of God's mercy and love. I entered recovery a long time ago, but it has not been a path of total abstinence or one without some incredible emotional pain. I have wondered, "Why me?" Sometimes I feel very distant from God. But when I am able to be silent and to quit talking *at* him, to begin to listen, I can feel his presence. And I hear again, "Nothing can separate you from my love for you."

> If I ascend to heaven, you are there; if I make my bed in Sheol, you are there....you knit me together in my mother's womb.
>
> PSALM 139:8, 13

God knit us together once, and God still holds us now. Hell is the relapse and all that brings with it. But by believing we belong to God we trust that God loves us, whether we are using or not! We are in relationship with God. Isn't this absolutely amazing? Isn't this spiritual healing?

Prayer

God certainly expects me to participate in this challenge. Part of the participation is to be in conversation with him; in other words, we're invited to pray. Sometimes even being open to praying feels like a risk. As Nancy says, she has no big theological thoughts but discovered that when she says, "Just sit here with me for a minute," she feels God next to her.

God expects us to be active in all aspects of recovery. He gives me freedom to put into action the opportunities he places in front of me as well as freedom to decline his gracious (grace filled) invitation to this gift of recovery—this gift of spiritual health. I can choose to live in bleakness and despair, or I can live in hope and joy.

Hope and Joy

Hope is a gift from God. It's very different from shallow optimism. Often we use the word *hope* to convey wishful thinking. We say, "I hope I can pay the rent....I hope the charges will be dropped....I hope he calls today....I hope I get that new job."

When we have hope in *sustained* recovery we have hope, but not for something *we create*, but a hope *we receive* in faith. To have hope is to have a future. Even if that future has some difficulties and failures, hope is a belief that the future will be good.

Because hope is a gift from God, hope contains a strong confidence in God's promises. He will use everything to accomplish his gracious purpose in our lives.

If we live in hope, when we get lost in a relapse or when the bottom drops out of our lives, we refuse to give in to despair. We remember those promises. We remember to be still and to listen, as Nancy does, for his voice. We remember to place our despair, our shame under the cloak of his grace. This new hope, this trust in his promises is a refuge.

He has promised a blessed future.

Bless the Lord, O my soul, and all that is within me, bless
his holy name.
Bless the Lord, O my soul, and do not forget
all his benefits—
who forgives all your iniquity,
who heals all your diseases,
who redeems your life from the Pit,
who crowns you with steadfast love and mercy,
who satisfies you with good as long as you live so that
your youth is renewed like the eagle's.

PSALM 103:1-5

It is that kind of hope out of which joy is born.

Joy is not a superficial happiness. Joy is the sense that God's healing really touches our lives. We begin to see evidence of that healing in the healing of our broken selves and in the relationships we thought were broken forever. Ultimately it is God's healing of our relationship with Him that brings us the real joy of healing other relationships. And of our recovery. We are invited to return home again...and again and again. Blessed by God.

Things to *Think About*

1. *Given that your addiction is a chronic disease, what changes will you make in your lifestyle of recovery ?*
2. *What specific area of your health can you improve within a month? How?*
3. *Where is there spiritual healing in your recovery?*

CHAPTER • 6

A: Anger and Abuse

*I*f you are reading this book, it is likely you are a woman concerned about your own substance use or some other behavior that needs to change. Or you're working with someone who is challenged by these issues. Research tells us it's likely that eight out of every ten women with substance abuse issues have experienced some kind of abuse—physical, sexual, emotional, mental. No wonder they are angry!

Of course, not all anger is connected with abuse. However, a majority of women I have worked with have experienced both abuse and anger. They may label it frustration, irritation, resentment, or fear. A woman's "official diagnosis" might say she has depression or anxiety and she often uses drugs and alcohol repeatedly to numb the memories and the pain. In this chapter we will weave the anger, the abuse, and, ultimately, the recovery together.

Woman A sits in a group and cries quietly as woman B risks disclosing some traumatic abusive experience she had as a child. Woman B pauses and then says, "These feelings of terror that I had as a little kid keep coming back! Now I'm an adult, but sometimes I feel like that child again!" Several women in the group brush away tears. At some point the counselor asks woman B, "I wonder if you aren't angry about this horrific experience?" Woman B seems almost stunned as if it has never occurred to her to be angry about it. But once the emotion of anger is named, she recognizes it, as do many of the other group members. The entire group likely erupts into tears of rage and disbelief. Each recognizes she is not alone The courage to *name* injustices from the past can most often happen within the safety of a women's group where the woman is "permitted" to rage at the perpetrator or at her own mother for not protecting her or believing her. Over time, she begins to realize it is *not* her fault. She learns that anger and rage are not only common but valid responses to abuses of trust.

Remember Nancy's story? Remember the sexual abuse she suffered by her father, brother, and husband? The emotional abuse from her mother? The way her employer and coworkers abused her? And, of course, the way she abused her own body over many years. It's very likely you have your own story.

THE POWER OF WORDS

Before we get started on the causes and "cures" for destructive anger, I want to share something very important with you that I learned from a workshop participant. During a particular professional presentation I had emphasized that one of the first steps to healing from anger was when a woman could "admit" she had been a victim of abuse. I stressed the importance of this admission (versus denial) as a first step in healing. After the workshop one of the professional participants approached me and said, "I wish you would consider changing your use of the word 'admit.' It would be much more helpful to use the word 'acknowledge.'" She continued, "When we ask patients to 'admit' they were victims of abuse, we imply they have done something wrong. At some level we are saying we blame them for the abuse. Victims of abuse have not done anything wrong. We ask people to 'admit' they ran a red light or maybe even 'admit' they cheated on their income tax. When we 'admit' something we say we are guilty of something.

But people who have been abused have not done anything wrong. They are not guilty of anything they have to 'admit' to." She went on. "Yes, it is very important they find a place where they can begin to *acknowledge* what happened and begin to heal but they do not have to *admit* to anything."

I am grateful for learning, once again, how powerful words can be. They shape and frame the way we think about things, the way we feel about ourselves. *Admit. Acknowledge.* As we listen, we learn.

In this chapter we explore what anger looks like, what role it takes in our lives, and how we might come to respond to it in a constructive way. And we need to understand that many women's anger is shaped by their own experience of abuse.

There are, of course, many reasons for women's anger, and we will think about how anger develops, from a relational perspective—and often from abuse in significant relationships (*name*). We will consider what to do with the anger—other than our usual pattern of covering it with alcohol/drugs/eating/cutting (*transform*). And ultimately, and so vital to sustained recovery, we let ourselves be led into a more gentle way of being. We will consider forgiveness as essential to that gentle way of being (*sustain*).

NAME

When I first started presentations on these STIGMA issues, I was uncomfortable that the issue of anger came as the final topic of the workshop. Although it is the last letter of the acronym, STIGMA, it underlies and permeates every other topic. To begin to heal, we need to consider where the anger comes from and how the pain lives and spirals back and forth within us now. We need to *name* it.

Where does anger come from?

One time anger gets triggered is when what we have come to

believe "should" occur in our lives doesn't occur. It can also be triggered when someone or something threatens our self-esteem or self-image. It can be triggered when we feel trapped in a role or a destructive relationship. It can be triggered when words demean us. It can be triggered when a loss feels unfair. It can be triggered when medical issues seem overwhelming. And it can be triggered by abuse. It is useful to look at these causes to understand that our anger does not just come out of the blue. There is a cause. We are not bad women for feeling anger. When we begin to understand the source, we have a better chance of examining it and doing something productive with it.

Our Values Versus Our Reality

Think about your own anger. Think about the anger you hear when you and your women friends are talking. The anger I hear is often about injustice: a boyfriend or husband who betrayed her, a credit card company extracting outrageous fees, an inability to pay all the bills even while working two jobs, being talked down to at work or home.

Anger gets triggered when the events in our lives do not match our values. The Stone Center indicates that the beliefs most associated with women's angry responses are those related to the personal standards or values we believe in. A woman's anger is generated around how those values are honored or not honored in our life experiences. Life is fair when people:

- Make moral decisions
- Care about each other
- Sacrifice to take care of others
- Don't hurt each other
- Share power equally
- Assume responsibility for their behavior

When these standards are operating in our daily experiences, life seems good. But when other people behave in ways that do not match these values, we become angry. Life seems very unfair. The values we have come to believe as just and honorable are not met.

These values are part of the guidelines we set for ourselves and for our relationships with others. We are angry because something we strongly believe in has been dishonored.

Our Standards

In addition to values in our lives we also have standards we hope to live by. In our reality we expect others to live by those standards also. When we don't live by those standards and when others betray them, we become angry. Those standards revolve around power, justice, and responsibility.

Power

As most of us would agree, men continue to hold the ultimate power over many situations in our lives and in our society. It is usually men who make decisions about money, division of duties, and laws. Of course great progress has been made with more women in administrative positions, in the U.S. Congress, and on the Supreme Court. But we often feel powerless if we can't make things happen in our personal lives and our jobs. When we can't, we often become angry.

Justice

Misuse of power often leads to injustices of betrayal and disrespect. If a friend discloses a confidence I have shared, I feel betrayed. If a spouse has an affair, I feel betrayed. Promises have been broken. I am angry!

Even when we are engaged in activities that support our own standards and values, some circumstances can feel unfair. I spoke with a neighbor recently. She has no substance use issues, but she feels something is unfair. For years she has been fundraising and doing bake sales and working very hard to raise scholarship money for her teenagers to be able to travel with school groups. They have gone to China and Europe and other exotic places. The teenagers are great kids and work hard themselves to be eligible for these trips. They participate in the fundraising. But she said to me as we talked at the mailbox, "When is it going to be my turn? When do *I* get to go on a trip?" It was unspoken but clear: This not fair!

I would guess if I asked her if she was angry, she would probably say, "Oh no. I just get a little frustrated at times." Often as women, we have difficulty acknowledging we are angry. After all, what is the usual term for an angry woman? Bitch? Harpy? Why do we fear letting people we care about know there is a situation that seems unfair—that angers us? What do we think will happen if we share that irritation or anger? Will they discover another part of us that we feel we must keep hidden? What happens to this kind of resentment? Do we use the alcohol or drugs to soothe it? I'm not my neighbor's therapist, but at some point we may have a conversation about what happens to us if we let feelings of unfairness build and never confront the anger behind it.

Responsibility

Your husband refuses to watch the children so you can go to aftercare. Or maybe he arrives home so you can get to the meeting, but when you return from the meeting the kids are still up and the kitchen is a mess. He does not accept responsibility for his part of the relationship. You want him to change and he doesn't. This lack of responsibility is a real trigger for our anger and resentments. We expect the significant people in our lives to act responsibly. We expect them to share in the work and play of keeping our lives moving in a positive direction.

Our issue here is not about who cleans up the kitchen. It's about the basic attitude that defines gender roles, about the sharing of the responsibility in a home. How do we begin to have that conversation in a meaningful way that respects each other's contributions? Way too often we get into our ineffective communication. We don't clearly ask for what we need. We think if they loved us they would know what we need. We fail to deeply listen to what the other is saying. We spend the time we should be listening in coming up with our own position, our own argument. And we leave the conversation angry. We will talk more about how we manage this kind of anger in *transform*, but it is helpful here to remember our previous use of the word "responsible." Responsibility does not mean I have to take on the load of the whole situation myself. The word can be broken into two pieces—"able" to "respond." I can be clear about identifying my needs, and I can ask for help. I am in a relationship. It is a mutual situation. In responsible communication we say things like, "I really need your help here. I want things to be better between us, and I need to get to a meeting. How can we make it work for both of us?"

Abuse

Any kind of abuse is the ultimate violation of the values of power, justice, and responsibility in any relationship. If the abuse occurs during childhood, a young girl lacks any sense of standards from which to measure relationships. She feels *powerless.* If she "tells," she runs the risk of losing the relationship with the perpetrator or suffering the loss of other relationships. She may fear for herself or others' safety if she tells. She knows at her core that this is not just. She wants to feel safe, but all she feels is fear. There is a total lack of responsibility from those who should love and protect her. She thinks she has no power and is truly adrift. She does not learn what to expect from herself and from others. So she relieves her anxiety by using drugs or alcohol, by bingeing and purging, or by cutting herself. When the addiction becomes active, the anger is turned against ourselves. It gets all tied up in our guilt and shame— our disempowerment, our injustice, and our irresponsibility. We violate every measure we value, and we judge ourselves. We stay in other abusive relationships because that is what feels normal. That's what we expect. In a bizarre twist, it feels comfortable. The cycle of addiction and abuse continues...and escalates. And so does our anger.

Anger and Self-esteem

As we consider what triggers our personal anger as women, one reality to keep in mind is that, in general, society holds male values in higher esteem than female values. For example, the male characteristics of "doing and knowing things" is generally held in higher value than female characteristics of "kindness, consideration, and friendliness." Society underscores this with higher salaries for engineers (knowing) or construction workers (doing) than for nurses, counselors, or social workers (kindness, consideration, and friendliness). If we choose to be in one of the lower-salaried, nurturing careers, we foster our self-esteem by maintaining a sense of competence and mastery. I have a friend who was teacher of the year for her state—a real master. Her husband, a very high–salaried engineer, frequently reminds her that he brings home 90 percent of the family income. Though he gives verbal lip service to her gifts as mother and teacher, at the bottom line in any conversation regarding family spending decisions such as family vacations, new cars, or a new TV, he reminds her that his income has controlling power. She is livid!

Besides anger, depression is another emotion connected with low self-esteem that comes from feeling devalued. There is an old saying in psychiatry that "depression is anger turned inward."

For example, Melanie was a client who countered everything said by anyone else with the opposite opinion. Initially, I thought she was just a very negative person. If someone in the group had good news, Melanie could find all the reasons it wasn't going to work. If someone had bad news, she had worse news. When she received a suggestion regarding one of her concerns from a group member, there was always a "Yes, but...."

The more I listened to Melanie, the more I realized she was depressed. Her depression came out in her angry voice and interactions. Her self-esteem was so threatened that, no matter what the situation might be, she felt she would not emerge as competent. Or responsible. She was critical of most people and, in fact, had lost several jobs because of her critical nature. She thought people deliberately provoked her, and she continuously played events over and over in her head to the point of obsession. Once we began to focus on her poor self-esteem and her perceptions that others saw her as "less than," she began to hear her outside voice as others heard it and could finally begin to name the anger within.

RESPONSES TO ANGER

What happens to the anger and the pain that comes with the anger? Where does it go? Generally in theoretical discussions of anger a woman's responses are placed in two major categories: "anger-in"—suppressed anger—and "anger-out"—expressed anger.

Unfortunately society generally does not tolerate a woman's expression of anger. As we said, if she expresses anger, "She's a first-class bitch!" If she holds it in, "She has the patience of a saint." If you hear sainthood equated with suppression of anger long enough, you begin to think anger must be a sin. A "good" woman doesn't show anger. Sour anger goes underground. This repressed anger becomes distorted and often manifests itself as an illness.

The illness might be anxiety, substance abuse, migraine headaches, obesity, self-abuse, or a host of other illnesses. The woman might request and receive tranquilizers for the early anger or "anxiety." We are very good at covering up our symptoms with drugs. Early on, our substance abuse, migraine headaches, eating disorders, and self-abuse don't bother anyone else, and they work to calm the anger. The quieter the disease, the more the woman is looked on as virtuous. We are willing to repress the anger because we fear losing relationships. We act as though we are without needs, and anger finds a home in our bodies.

When anger resides in our bodies, there can be physical manifestations. In the previous chapter we talked about the medical consequences of substance abuse. There are also serious medical consequences of unresolved anger. Anger sets off a physical chain reaction. It starts in our nervous system and our cardiovascular, immune, digestive, and sensory systems. Some research indicates repressed anger is the chief toxic component in diseases of our coronary artery system. As we have indicated, heart disease is the number one killer of women. Our immune systems also suffer with repressed anger as evidenced in decreased immune markers. When we are upset, we get more colds, more flu. Our immune system is suppressed when our anger is suppressed. Our digestive system can be affected by anger leading to upset stomach, ulcers, and colitis. When we say we were so angry we "couldn't think straight," we are saying the anger affected our senses and our brains. People who are angry or tense often reach for a cigarette. Smokers report that a cigarette soothes their anger, calms them—an indirect link to quieting anger through endorphins released in the brain. Too many of us know the quieting effect of that first shot, or hit, or pint of ice cream, or cut.

Because it appears there are so many negative consequences to suppressed anger, it is essential to learn the healthy options. As we talked about previously in the discussion of stress, we need to pay attention to where our bodies are tense, where they are holding the anger. We pay attention to the words going around in our thoughts. We acknowledge that a particular situation makes us angry. It's not irritation. It's not frustration. It is anger! And we can express it in ways that don't destroy our relationships. We learn not to save it up and then dump it all over the wrong situation. We *transform* the angry feelings, the angry words, the anger held inside into expressions of our values, our sense of power, justice, and responsibility.

TRANSFORM

To move anger from an emotion that frightens us, one we fear will end in a broken relationship, or an emotion we use to abuse ourselves, it is necessary to take care of ourselves in different ways. Once we discharge the initial tension of anger (through breathing, counting to ten, quick walk, tense/relax muscles) it is essential to dig deeper and explore the situations that stimulate our anger. We consider the pain that has been imprinted deep inside. We begin to acknowledge that this event, situation, and pain are really a part of our lives. It really did happen! With an acceptance of our reality we begin to transform the control the anger has over us. We begin to answer the question, "What do I want to feel instead of the anger and rage?"

Discharge of the Initial Energy

Claire arrived at the workshop late. She made her presence felt as she found the coffee, hung up her coat, and settled herself in a chair. When it was her turn to introduce herself, her tone was angry. "This has been one of the worst weeks since I got into recovery three years ago. I am so angry! My house was broken into and I was robbed this week. I feel like I have been violated. Not only were my credit cards all gone and some jewelry but my sense of safety is gone."

As the day progressed, Claire continued to talk about this robbery, and everyone sensed that the storm of tension that surrounded her in the morning began to diminish. At the first break another participant invited her to take a walk down the country road near where the meeting was being held. She returned visibly less stressed, even with a slight smile on her face. She continued to talk of the robbery as the group discussed the STIGMA issues. She frequently mentioned the injustice and unfairness of the situation…the work to get new credit cards, fix the broken screen and windows, clean up the mess of the looting. She had not been able to sleep alone in the house since the robbery so she had asked an adult daughter to come stay with her, but the daughter had declined, and Claire was angry about that. The tension in her body was evident each time her anger resurfaced. We brought that to her awareness. "The least she could have done was come stay and help me clean up." We talked a bit more about the relationship with her daughter. Clearly there was some history there, and the group suggested maybe she just needed to step away from talking with her daughter for a few days while the crisis of the robbery was so fresh. In spite of her anger, Claire had been able to take the steps she needed to take: cancel credit cards, obtain new ones, get the window and screen repaired, talk with the police. She had separated what had seemed overwhelming into achievable tasks.

We talked about her urge to drink during the hours and days after the robbery. She said, "You know, it crossed my mind, but I knew I had to be clear in my thinking as I worked on this. I was worried though about this weekend. I had a thought that I deserved a couple of good shots once I got through the worst of it. It would help me release some of my anger. But I came here instead. I knew that if I came to this workshop and talked about it, the thought of taking a drink would lose some of its power."

Claire's story is a good example of some of the ways we might initially deal with anger that arises because of a particular situation. She thought about her circumstances and initiated some problem solving. She called on someone for help, and when that person wasn't available she had other names and phone numbers available. She thought she might know who had committed the robbery, but she didn't go right over and confront him. She left that to the police. She did not react. She had a plan. She was not helpless. She began to reclaim a small piece of her balance and her power. An anger management plan is essential for anyone in recovery because healing takes a long time, and, without a plan, we set ourselves up for relapse.

Anger at Different Levels

Some anger is aroused by incidents we might not see as consequential, and some anger is so deeply embedded that it is hard to name. Like my neighbor, we often minimize anger by saying we are "frustrated" or "upset" or even "freaked out." But we need to think about how these feelings develop and how they make an imprint on the ways we think and behave.

When we're bent on *transforming* our lives, it is crucial we recognize and identify anger as soon as possible. It is also helpful to name the trigger, the standard we want to live by, that has been betrayed. Do we feel powerless? Is the situation injustice or unfairness? By naming it, we have a chance to begin to understand our response and formulate a plan to deal with it. By knowing where it comes from, what value of ours has been violated, we validate the emotion and the anger does not take control. We give ourselves the power to do something different.

Probably the angriest client I ever worked with was a nurse from a large university hospital. Diane had endured a long history of physical and sexual abuse from her father. She raged against her mother for not protecting her, and Diane's rage was easily reignited whenever she thought someone treated her unfairly. Her drug abuse had resulted in her reassignment from an intensive care unit to a floor nurse position. She was incensed and humiliated. She felt a loss of power, unfairness, and injustice. After her reassignment she would sometimes come to counseling with outrageous stories of what she had angrily said to a patient or a colleague. But I wasn't her nurse manager; I was her therapist, so I listened and worked with her to make sense of what had really happened in a given situation. We talked about her perception of the conflict. After much work with both her nurse manager and myself, one day she was able to say, "You know what I think I finally figured out? When I feel myself get really angry, before I mouth off, I need to ask myself, 'Is this the hill I want to die on?' If it isn't really that important

I need to take a deep breath and walk away." It was the first time I had heard "the hill" example, and I have since used it myself and with others.

You'll begin to notice, that by taking time out for the self-talk and the muscle-relaxing exercises we talked about with stress, or deep breathing, walking, or visualizations, the initial anger-arousal subsides. When that anger-arousal subsides there is time to reflect on the situation and put our anger in a larger context. Sometimes informal self-talk such as "Wow! Where did that come from?" or "What just happened here?" releases some of the tension. By identifying the value or standard that has been demeaned I can better understand myself and see the world a little more clearly.

As Claire was able to share with us later in the day of the workshop, she felt such anger at the robber because of the threat to her personal safety (powerlessness). She had endured a physically abusive marriage for fifteen years, and only in recovery had she found her own apartment and begun to feel some peace and security. The robbery recreated that sense of dread. It wasn't only her jewelry and credit cards that had been stolen. It was her power and control.

Claire wasn't my client, but if she were I would encourage her to continue the work of increasing her awareness of situations in which she feels a burst of anger. I would suggest she journal daily and talk about the feelings triggered by the many aspects of the robbery. I would talk to her about the relationship with her daughter. I would ask whether she would be willing to explore some of her old issues and look at where she is with them in the here and now. I would encourage her to reflect on what value of hers had been slighted or snubbed by her daughter's unwillingness to come the night of the robbery. Is it the powerlessness, the injustice, the irresponsibility, or all three?

Later I would encourage her to assess several other things related to her anger, which you also might find useful:

- The frequency of the anger. How often do you get angry? Write it down in a daily journal. Are you surprised at how often?
- The intensity. On a scale of one to ten how strong is the anger? Is it just an irritation, or is it more like rage?
- The duration. Does it last a long time? Do you hold onto it, or does it pass pretty quickly? How do you know?
- How do you express it? Yell? Cry? Withdraw? Throw things? Or say "I need to get back to you about this"?

When we honestly assess our anger, we learn how we function and ultimately how to modify our reactions. Our "normal" reactions to the anger often set up situations that simply feed on themselves. I get angry, I yell, and the situation escalates. Or I get angry, I withdraw, and the isolation and sense of powerlessness increases.

Empowerment

Think of Nancy, the plumber. She believed she had no power in her parents' home and no power in her marriage. Once she stopped the drugs, once the mind-numbing began to clear, once she named the anger (in her paintings and in discussions with Joe and me) and the pain that came from a lifetime of abuse, her pain began to diminish. She found a new job, one that gave her health benefits and would provide some retirement income (power). She began to verbalize her opinion about things in the house, with her in-laws, and at work. Remember the story of the coworkers who were harassing her? She found her voice, her power, and confronted the situation (justice). No one gave her new power. By naming the injustice, she found the power within herself. It had been there all along. She also was empowered in the relationships that were proving to be safe, supportive, and mutual as she learned to use her voice.

The slow process of empowerment came strongly in her spiritual therapy. She began to trust the relationship with Joe enough to discuss her spiritual feelings. She began to name her anger at God. She brought her paintings and her journals. Joe helped her recognize the patterns of anger and hurt that she felt from the abuse and rejection by her parents. In a very significant ongoing dialogue they explored the way her parents and grandparents expressed anger. She could see the family patterns. The way she thought of herself began to change. She realized her family had spoken to each other like this for generations—maybe those hurtful words were not about her. Maybe she wasn't stupid. Maybe she didn't stink.

She began to understand that her abuse of drugs and alcohol was a way to deal with the pain. She began to understand she was not to blame for her father's abuse and abandonment. She had been emotionally abandoned by those who were responsible to protect her. She had survived in all of this pain. She was powerful.

Nancy has worked at this for years. First she stood up for herself at work with the coworkers who were harassing her. Next she stood up to her family when they accused a relative of abuse and she thought there was another side to the story. She was able to disagree even if it meant she might incur their anger. She risked a new relationship with her husband through finding her voice. Then she and her husband resolved the issue of scattering David's ashes. She was able to express her anger in each of these situations by naming the anger, discharging the energy, and discussing the emotion and the situation. Whenever she called Joe, often ranting and raving, he explored the hurt with her by asking:

- How did this event relate to things she cared about, her values?
- What was her fear?
- Were there other ways to look at the situation?
- What might she want to say or do about it?

Nancy confronted the critical issue of the distribution of her son's ashes after her success with her anger at work and her anger with relatives. It is not unusual that expressing anger is more difficult with those to whom we feel closest. Women are often most reluctant to express anger within the family circle. Why? We don't want to lose the relationship. We fear that, if we express our legitimate anger, they will leave. Maybe they won't leave literally, but we fear they will leave by silence or isolation. In her therapy, Nancy had the chance to role-play what she wanted to say to her husband, to hear some possible responses he might have, to look at alternative ways of expressing her anger, to consider what he might be feeling about the situation. These were strategies that helped her explore the here and now in relation to the past. This kind of examination gave her a safe space to tolerate the anger and pain.

By expressing this anger and pain about her husband's lack of communication, Nancy was also able to connect this pain with the core issue of a lifetime of loss, hurt, and not being heard. By talking about these feelings, Nancy moved further along in her grief process. Finally, she was able to talk again about the death of her son and what that loss meant to her at the center of her being.

Something Other Than the Anger and Pain

In all of these chapters we talked about our power to change our behavior and to change the way we think about particular people, places, and things. We felt powerless for so long in the active addiction. However, once we empower ourselves to change behaviors related to the addiction (such as staying away from the bars or the crack dealer or finding people who can help obtain food stamps or help get some job training) we realize we are *not* powerless. The addiction took away power. Recovery, a new way of thinking and being, gives it back.

As we learned in the Medical Aspects chapter, we have the option to change our thinking and feeling regarding our emotions. With a few challenging questions we might explore other factors that could affect a given situation. For example, think about what might have been going on with Nancy's husband and his desire to scatter their son's ashes. Did he just want to get on with the task? What about *his* grief, his loss, his pain? Anger and pain lock us in an emotional vise of reaction rather than allowing us power to alter what we have always done.

Our ability to finally name the anger, to explore the pain, to feel the fear, to examine the trap of addiction leads us to the reality of our experience. Nancy acknowledged the horror of her childhood. She drew and talked about the fear and pain. She was able to connect the fear and pain of childhood with the fear and pain in her marriage. She began to recognize the impact of the anger. "This is how I reacted when I was angry year after year....This is where the anger keeps tripping me up now in my life, in my relationships, in my recovery." Acceptance is not defeat. Acceptance is not loss. Acceptance is the ability to acknowledge the reality of our past.

New Normal

In the book *Amish Grace* (see Resources), a book about the shooting deaths of little girls in Nickel Mines, Pennsylvania, there is a significant discussion of the Amish healing process. The authors showed how the Amish community was able to move through a traumatic event and into a "new normal." Understanding and accepting that life can never go back to what it was before the traumatic event is vital to healing.

Part of our new normal in recovery is an acceptance that we can never change the past. We can never have a different childhood. We can never get that job back. We *were* in jail. Those things occurred in our life. When we are able to name the pain of the past, of abuse or anger or loss, we transform it into a new normal. We are able to say, "Yes, that was part of my past. Whatever the consequences of that event were, and maybe still are, this is my life now."

What Instead?

In the long process of *transforming* these connected emotions of fear, sadness, shame, anger, and so forth a relevant question becomes, "What do I want to feel other than anger and pain?" When I was first asked that question, my initial response was, "I don't want to feel the guilt and shame anymore." My counselor pushed back gently and said, "I know that's what you *don't* want to feel, but what *do* you want to feel instead? With what do you want to replace the anger and guilt and shame?"

It took me a while to come up with the words that work for me as replacements, but once I heard them a place deep within me softened. I want to replace the anger and guilt and shame with a gentle life...a life of peacefulness, a life in which I am gentle with myself and gentle with others... a life that has moved from broken to blessed...a life in which I feel the gentle embrace of a loving God.

My friend, Karen Speerstra, described what I was feeling in a poem she calls "Gentle Me, Jesus":

Only you can keep surfaces from cracking;
Only you can keep edges from splintering.
Smooth me into sphere-shape,
Perfect like your own.
Round me when I turn rigid;
Bend me when I am boxed.
Circle me with your love.
Gentle me, Jesus.

SUSTAIN

The pursuit of the gentle life is a crucial part of recovery. This isn't easy for most of us because we may still harbor so much anger. Some person or some situation has caused us unbelievable pain. However, somewhere within us is a growing awareness that, like a boulder in the middle of the road, this anger of ours obstructs our way forward. It trips us up time after time. Forgiveness is essential to taking back the power that we have given to the anger. Forgiveness is core to a gentle life. Forgiveness is fundamental to *sustained* recovery. Forgiveness is part feeling blessed by God.

Forgiveness

Forgiveness, like recovery, is a process. That's what makes it so hard to define. It involves overcoming resentment, and it takes a very long time. Most writers who attempt to discuss forgiveness do so by saying it has dimensions—meaning there are several different angles from which we can look at this word.

In a medical sense, forgiveness reduces anger, depression, anxiety, and fear. It is tied up with reducing our stress and has benefits for the cardiovascular and immune systems. Theologians of various denominations concentrate on scriptural examples of God's forgiveness. Their perspective says God does not hold on to his anger at us for our many transgressions. In theological discussion of forgiveness, our guilt and shame are relieved as we understand God's unconditional love for us. We are not asked to forgive ourselves but to understand and believe in God's forgiveness of us.

Each of these dimensions is pertinent to a discussion of forgiveness in our STIGMA model of recovery and healing. Our Self-image requires an understanding of God's forgiveness. Our Traditional role requires the interpersonal forgiveness of others and our understanding of why that may come slowly. Ineffective communication requires the healing of words spoken by us and others in relationship. Grief and loss require the spiritual forgiveness centered in God's promise that he is always with us. Medical consequences are relieved by forgiveness. Anger and abuse require healing in all the dimensions of forgiveness—medical, social, personal, and theological.

A Model of Forgiveness

Because forgiveness is essential to the work involved in our progress to resolve each of the STIGMA issues of recovery, there are features of forgiveness that are helpful for us to consider. One of the more recent, profound writers about forgiveness is Bishop Desmond Tutu. Bishop Tutu, a black man imprisoned, beaten, and abused for years by the white government of South Africa, has dedicated much of his post-prison life to teaching and writing extensively about forgiveness. The following discussion uses some vital points from Bishop Tutu's book, *No Future Without Forgiveness* (see References). These points guide our thinking to further our understanding of what forgiveness might mean for us as we work on our anger and forgiveness in recovery.

"Forgive and forget" is what we are often encouraged to do. But that is not possible—at least the forget part. In fact, we need to remember.

Particularly in a situation such as abuse, we need to remember. We do not want to "let the atrocities happen again." Abuse often continues in families almost as a legacy, not because people necessarily want to be cruel but often because they themselves do not know how to love. They have not learned other ways to handle their own anger and hurt. If we "forget" our hurt we run the risk of being stuck in the same destructive behaviors as our perpetrators. When recovering persons, both men and women, tell the stories of the childhood abuse they have suffered, the perpetrator has often been a parent. By remembering the hurt we know our parenting must interrupt the cycle. As women in recovery we know it must stop with us. We must not forget.

Sometimes we don't forgive because we can't acknowledge that someone has hurt us. We deny we are angry because to acknowledge the hurt feels like giving the abuser the power to hurt us again. But by denying the hurt and anger, we continue to push it deep inside. Festering there, it waits to attack us and others in destructive ways and at destructive times.

Sometimes hurts really are more of an irritation or a nuisance than a horrid, deep hurt. It is helpful to sort out those feelings and bear the lighter annoyance with some amount of grace. Otherwise forgiveness is trivialized or consumes our daily conversations. The hurts we are talking about here are the ones that wound us deeply. The sorts Desmond Tutu experienced: purposeful, long-standing, and brutal.

Forgiveness is not forgetting, nor is it overlooking or excusing.
In fact forgiveness is just the opposite. Although we may forgive
someone, we still hold that person accountable for his or
her behavior.

In the example of Amish forgiveness we talked about in the Transform section and a new normal, the Amish did not condone the shootings or excuse them. To excuse them would have meant there would be no consequences. The Amish believe in consequences. In the case of the shootings the perpetrator committed suicide immediately. Many of the Amish acknowledged that his immediate death made the process of forgiveness easier. In general, they leave the consequences of such unlawful acts to the legal process of the state. They also acknowledged that the process of forgiveness was less painful because the perpetrator was not of their "community." Had he been Amish, he would have violated the core of their values and standards.

Some of the people caught up in that Amish community tragedy actually went to the perpetrator's family bearing grace and love. Many of us find that incomprehensible. We're immersed in an aggressive culture focused in large part on resentment, retaliation, and revenge. Movies, television, and computer games emphasize the legitimacy of violence as a way of managing anger and disagreements. We teach our boys to stand up for themselves and fight for their honor. We teach our girls to suppress their anger and be sweet and compliant. Rarely do we teach the process of forgiveness or even hold forgiveness as a value to be honored.

Forgiveness is an essential doctrine of the Amish faith. They recite the Our Father prayer with the admonition to "forgive us our trespasses as we forgive those who trespass against us" in their morning and evening prayers. Schoolchildren read lessons and learn prayers that teach lessons of forgiveness. Whereas in other religions people believe God's forgiveness is unconditional, the Amish truly believe that to be forgiven of their sins they must first forgive others.

As we think about forgiveness in recovery, we know that, if you were abused by a family member or someone you trusted, forgiveness is a terribly difficult process. Those perpetrators were of "our community." The abuse violates a confidence that betrays security and safety, both basic needs for growth of personality and relationships. Instead of loving and protecting us, they broke us.

Forgiveness makes every effort to walk in the shoes of those who have inflicted pain upon us and, as a result, develop a sense of empathy to try to understand the pressures that have shaped them.

Fifteen years into her recovery, Nancy was asked if she had forgiven her parents. She said, "Yes—it wasn't easy. I've looked at things I've learned and I feel so sorry that they never learned what I did....She [mother] was never loved....When Dad crosses my mind, I'm sorry he never knew me....When I think of my brother, he's an old man now. I just put it aside. I don't need to hold onto it."

This is an incredible statement of forgiveness. Through work and prayer Nancy has been able to look at the tragic childhood and lives of her parents. She understands that her willingness to explore their histories has given her insight into their woundedness. She has talked and cried, written about them, and drawn them. Finally, she is able to "feel sorry" that they never learned what she has learned. She says she used to curse at Jesus about her life. Now if she feels the old hurt and pain, she prays, "OK Jesus, let's talk about this." A new normal. What grace!

Forgiveness is a long process. Often we think we have moved along in the process only to have the anger triggered again by something that happens today. However, we don't need to judge the quality of our forgiveness by whether we have forgotten or whether we at times remember with feelings of the old anger and pain. Even the Amish say it is work that never ends. The concept of forgiveness outlined in *Amish Grace* says forgiveness comes in two stages. First there is the decision to forgive, and then later comes the emotional forgiveness.

Forgiveness means giving up the desire for revenge. As difficult as that may be to do, in the end it frees us from something that could easily poison our soul.

The decision to forgive indicates a promise not to act with revenge and not to avoid the person who has committed the abuse. We let go of the right to pay back. This is a difficult decision but one that essentially says, "I will not get back at you nor will I close off communication between us." Anger and bitterness may remain, but there is a conscious decision not to act on them. We all know families who have not spoken to certain members for years. They have cut off communication, and thus they have cut off any chance of reconciliation or forgiveness.

The initial decision neither to retaliate nor to close off communication gives a better chance for the later "emotional" forgiveness to emerge. Emotional forgiveness means that we replace the angry feelings of hostility or hatred with more grace-filled feelings. Emotional forgiveness may have to happen over and over again as memories and situations reproduce angry feelings. It takes a great deal of work as we have said so often in this book. This work proceeds with less pain and more joy when done with someone who supports you and empathizes with you—a person such as a counselor or pastor.

Forgiveness may feel like a loss. A woman may think that even to consider forgiveness betrays her own self-respect. It makes her angry all over again. They don't deserve to be forgiven!

It is helpful to acknowledge those angry feelings because to repress or deny them robs us of the possibility of growth. With awareness of the feelings we have the chance to work them through a little at a time. With God's grace over time there is just a slight difference in the intensity of the feelings, and we find ourselves less and less overwhelmed. You can't be conned into forgiving. It must be authentic. You can't deny the past pain, but you can come to realize this is the time for a new normal. You can also develop some understanding regarding the perpetrator's belief system—even if it seems evil. When we taste a food that is too bitter, we wash it out with clear water or something sweet. When we have the bitterness of anger, we must wash it out with different purer and cleaner thoughts.

In authentic forgiveness, the loss of bitter feelings and the need for revenge is replaced with a feeling of freedom. You can say, "This perpetrator no longer controls my feelings or my life. When I am able to forgive, I become the hero instead of the victim in this story. I'm now free to write the end of my story."

Please understand this: If there is to be a future to our recovery, forgiveness is absolutely necessary. Especially it is essential to our spiritual life. Forgiveness is absolutely necessary for our continued human existence in recovery and for our continued spiritual journey. We certainly may remember the abuse or betrayal, but it is how we choose to remember it that brings the healing. We acknowledge our own and others' frailties and vulnerability. With the beginnings of forgiveness we feel the divine mystery of this shift to compassion. We know we are blessed.

Tutu says when we are able to begin to forgive we obtain a future with freedom. Freedom to what? *Freedom to live life well.* Freedom to live life more as a gift than as a struggle because we know *we* are forgiven. Listen! "I, I am He who blots out your transgressions for my own sake, and I will not remember your sins" (Isaiah 43:25).

We are forgiven. Say it: "I am forgiven." We are given the

freedom to place our recovery in a spiritual life and move from broken to blessed. We are wrapped and held in a gentle spirituality, a relationship with God.

This gentle spirituality means I am open to everything that touches me. It is a gift from the Holy Spirit, a gift of grace, a gift of awareness. I live more fully, more boldly, and more freely, not as a struggle but as a gift. This gentle life, this spiritual life, is an awareness of the sacred. The continuous blessing of the sacred instills gentleness in the soul. In *sustained* recovery we become aware and attentive to that gentle divine presence in every aspect of our recovery. We move from broken by addiction to blessed by God.

I KNOW I AM BLESSED

In Self-image, blessedness comes with the focus of myself as deeply loved and cared for by God within the life given to me.

In Traditional roles, blessedness results from the experience of God in the sacrament of everydayness, knowing where I am at home.

In Ineffective communication, blessedness creeps in silently. It comes in listening, in really hearing the questions. It surges as an awakened source of energy and light. It is healing reflection in divine mystery.

In Grief and loss, blessed is the release of the burden of a heavy heart. It is movement into graciousness and joy. It is knowing God's forgiveness.

In Medical aspects, blessedness returns me to aliveness. It means placing my feelings, my illnesses, my sufferings back into God's grace. I see it in the process of recovery held in spirituality.

In Anger and abuse, blessedness presents a life of gentleness. It offers me a choice to move out of the shadow and into the light. It bestows on me the freedom of forgiveness. It gives me an attentiveness to the creative action of the divine in my life.

To live my recovery in blessedness means to risk living into an openness to God's divine promises of his unconditional love and his presence in my life. And to share that blessing with others.

Things to *Think About*

1. *What would you like to feel other than anger?*
2. *Keep a diary to assess your anger. Make notes of the frequency, intensity, duration, and expression of times you are aware of feeling angry.*
3. *How does forgiveness free you?*

Epilogue

Joe, Nancy's spiritual therapist, gives this presentation in work-shops we provide and to health care professionals, congregations, recovering women, and treatment centers. It is a powerful scriptural adaptation of centering a woman's recovery in her relationship with God. It is a beautiful summary of our discussion.

ADDICTION—SPIRITUALITY AND THE LOST DAUGHTER

By Joe Hauser

Spirituality lies at the core of recovery from addiction—any addiction. Jesus told a wonderful timeless story that illustrates this. In the fifteenth chapter of Luke it is called the parable of the Prodigal Son. But it could just as well be the Prodigal Daughter.

The story begins with this simple fact: the daughter is at home with her mother. We were all created to be at home with God: to experience the warmth and joy of the mother's house, to be embraced and loved as her children, to be at one with God and at one with ourselves and at one with others. This forms the basis of our spirituality. God has created us to live in relationship with her.

And while the wasteful, prodigal daughter was at home with her mother, that is, while she lived in a steady and committed relationship with her mom, her life was in balance and she experienced peace. But then she decided to leave. Why? Because she wanted to be her own boss—her own god. Her mother's house, she thought, has became too restrictive, too burdensome. Too many rules. I want to be free to live my life on my own terms. It's time I enjoyed life, live it to the fullest, and experience a real trip, she told herself.

That is what is so insidious about addiction. It seems to add more zest to life. And what's so bad about wanting to enjoy a rich life?

So, the daughter turned her back and walked down the road. Alcohol and drugs, she not only thought but really *believed*, made her feel good about herself. When we believe something long enough, it becomes the truth for us. And when it's "true," we don't challenge or question it.

The prodigal daughter was more relaxed. This is normal, she thought. I'm happy and like everybody else. But before long her addictive behavior started to take over. Soon everything in her life revolved around using. What she thought was making her free, instead, enslaved her. She hit bottom. Pretty soon she was eating with the pigs. "I've wasted my life!" she cried.

In a spiritual sense, our addictions make idolaters out of us. In other words, we worship a false god. False ideas. But any horrible situation can actually be a blessing. Often it is in our darkness, our most powerless, our own unmanageability, despair, and hopelessness that we become conscious of the presence of God and experience his grace.

What is grace? For the prodigal daughter *grace* was the mother refusing to give up on her. It was the mother inviting her to return home. It was the mother herself going out to look for her daughter.

And that is what grace is for us too. God stubbornly refuses to write us off. It is God in the person of Jesus Christ who enters our poverty and our brokenness so that we might enjoy the riches of God's love. There we are, wading through the slop and the dung of the pigs, and God takes us by the hand and says, "Come home."

As with the prodigal daughter, letting go of our addiction is scary. Can I live without it? Will I feel normal? Won't I be empty?

I could reform. I know my addiction causes health problems, family problems, financial problems. But I don't want any serious overhaul. No radical change! It's uncomfortable, but I'd rather put on a Band-Aid than face radical surgery.

But it's not reformation we need. It's transformation. God wants to *transform* our lives. He wants us to make friends with the emptiness we experience after we loosen the grip on our addiction(s). Why? Because that emptiness—as frightening and painful as it may be—gives God the opportunity to enter our lives and accomplish in them the miracle of transformation. God invites us home. God's gracious work remakes our lives.

Addiction breaks the prodigal daughter. But God can use the very thing that almost crushed and destroyed her to bring her back. The addiction, of course, remains. We never get rid of it. But through God's loving grace, it can be changed from something that makes life miserable to something that pulls us back to God. There we find strength, peace, hope, and perseverance.

Even though admitting she's taken a wrong turn and it feels very risky, the prodigal daughter gets up, dusts herself off, and says, "I'm going back to Mom."

And that's what recovery is. A homecoming. But to get there, we have to face the grief of giving up what has seemed so exciting and fun.

Homecoming is a lifelong process. And it's made more difficult by our conflicted hearts. Part of us wants wholeness, but another part of us is drawn toward our addiction. Every day we are confronted with this choice: Do I commit myself to my addictions or do I surrender to God?

There she is, all beaten up, broken, dirty, battered. She doesn't know what Mom's reaction is going to be. Is it even safe to return? Her suitcase is full of shame and guilt and hurts. She's filled with questions. Can I live with the void of not drinking? Of not using drugs? Is life even worth it without my addictions? Will I be able to adjust to living in my mother's house again? Will they even want me there?

But we hear her say, "I'm getting up. I will dust myself off and I will go home."

What a profound leap of faith this statement carries. It is spirituality at its deepest level.

And this decision to "go home" is one of the miracles of the recovery process.

And what happens? The mother is waiting for her daughter to return. She throws up her hands and runs out to greet her. That is grace. "Welcome home, dear one. It doesn't matter what you've done, what you look like, or even how you feel. You're home now."

God's love is unconditional, forgiving, affirming, and inviting. It never asks embarrassing questions such as, "What makes you think *you* have a right to be back here?" Even if the daughter's motive for returning may have been selfish. She had to return to survive. That's OK too. God never demands a pure heart before she throws her arms around us. And God will take us back no matter how many times we leave and return. Because of Jesus Christ's death and resurrection, we know this to be a fact. We're always welcome.

It's a beautiful scene, the mother and daughter together. But there is more to this drama than meets the eye. Note the daughter's response to her mother's welcome. It would seem that she almost struggles to pull away from her mom's embrace. She claims that she is no longer worthy to be called her daughter. She seeks to be punished for behaving so badly. Just make me a servant, she says. I don't deserve my old room back. Put me on restrictive probation.

But God doesn't operate like that. There is no payment to be made. Christ already did that. Now the prodigal daughter has to accept the fact that she already *is* forgiven. Done! Put away your pocketbook. It's free. All we need to do is surrender to this loving presence.

And that is the very core of our struggles with our recovery from addiction. It is the slow and difficult path from acceptance to surrender: from acceptance *of* grace to surrender *to* grace.

This is a move that enables us to answer the critical question "Who am I?" in a different way. Instead of "I am a worthless mess who has totally screwed up my life" it becomes "I am a beloved daughter of God—forgiven, accepted, loved, blessed, and infinitely precious."

The prodigal daughter knows she is really home when she is

- Willing to change and be changed
- Willing to forgive and accept herself
- Willing to take the responsibility for being a daughter in her mother's house

Recovery, then is a long, bumpy, stinky journey back to the mother's house. It is a path that involves both pain and healing, sadness and joy, slavery and freedom, light and darkness, failure and success. The way is marked by contradictions and paradoxes. But it is worth taking this path because it is filled with miracles and mysteries. It is a journey from being broken by addiction to being blessed by God. It is a journey home. Only one question remains: Will the prodigal daughter stay at home? Will you?

God's Promises

From Romans 8:

> Likewise the Spirit helps us in our weakness; for we do not
> know how to pray as we ought, but that very Spirit intercedes
> with sighs too deep for words. And God, who searches the

heart, knows what is the mind of the Spirit, because the Spirit intercedes for the saints according to the will of God.

26–27

What then are we to say about these things? If God is for us, who is against us? He who did not withhold his own Son, but gave him up for all of us, will he not with him also give us everything else? Who will bring any charge against God's elect? It is God who justifies. Who is to condemn? It is Christ Jesus, who died, yes, who was raised, who is at the right hand of God, who indeed intercedes for us.

31–34

No, in all these things we are more than conquerors through him who loved us. For I am convinced that neither death, nor life, nor angels, nor rulers, nor things present, nor things to come, nor powers, nor height, nor depth, nor anything else in all creation, will be able to separate us from the love of God in Christ Jesus our Lord.

37–38

References

Belenky, M. F., B. M. Clinchy, and N. R. Goldberger. 1986. *Women's ways of knowing*. New York: Basic Books.

Bergman, S. 1991. Excerpt from "Work in Progress"—Male Relational Dread. Wellesley, MA: The Stone Center, Wellesley College. www.samuelshem.com.

Bonhoeffer, D. 1954. *Life together*. Trans. J. W. Doberstein. San Francisco: Harper & Row.

Buechner, F. 1992. *Listening to your life*. San Francisco: Harper.

Cleveland Clinic. 2009. www.ClevelandClinic.org.

Gottman, J., and N. Silver. 1999. *The seven principles for making marriage work*. New York: Three Rivers Press.

Harvard Medical School. 2001. *Alcohol use and abuse*. Boston: Harvard Health Publications.

Interlandi, J. 2008. What addicts need. *Newsweek,* February 23.

Jordan, J. V., A. G. Kaplan, J. B. Miller, I. P. Stiver, and J. L. Surrey. 1991. *Women's growth in connection*. New York: The Guilford Press.

Kraybill, D. B., S. M. Nolt, and D. L. Weaver-Zercher. 2007. *Amish grace*. San Francisco: Jossey-Bass.

Lamott, A. 1993. *Operating instructions*. New York: Anchor Books.

Lemonick, M. P., and A. Park. 2007. The science of addiction. *Time,* January 23.

Lindbergh, A. M. 1975. *Gift from the sea*. New York: Pantheon Books.

The National Center on Addiction and Substance Abuse at Columbia University. 2006. *Women under the influence*. Baltimore: The Johns Hopkins University Press.

National Institute on Drug Abuse, National Institute on Alcohol Abuse and Alcoholism. 2007. *Addiction*. HBO series.

Norris, K. 1998. *The quotidian mysteries*. New York: Paulist Press.

Nouwen, H. J. M. 1993. *Life of the beloved*. New York: Crossroad Publishing Company.

Taylor, B. B. 1998. *Mixed blessings*. Cambridge, MA: Cowley Publications.

Tutu, D. 1999. *No future without forgiveness*. New York: Doubleday.

Westberg, G. E. 2004. *Good grief*. Minneapolis: Augsburg Fortress.

Additional Resources

SPIRITUALITY: ANY TITLES BY THESE AUTHORS

Buechner, F. 1991. *Telling secrets.* San Francisco: Harper Collins.

Lamott, A. 1999. *Traveling mercies.* New York: Anchor Books.

Norris, K. 1996. *Cloister walk.* New York: Riverhead Books.

Nouwen, H. 1996. *Life of the beloved.* New York: Crossroad Publishing Company.

Taylor, B. B. 1998. *Mixed blessings.* Cambridge, MA: Cowley Books.

Music from The Brothers at Weston Priory. www.westonpriory.org.

Also, search the Liguori Publications Web site (www.liguori.org) for books, pamphlets, and music on many spiritual issues. It also has a meditation thought for the day. The *Liguorian* magazine Web site (www. liguorian.org) has articles and other information on spiritual issues.

SUBSTANCE ABUSE

The Cleveland Clinic has a great Web site for information on many diseases. www.clevelandclinic.org.

The HBO series *Addiction* is a wealth of information and resources on the disease of addiction with focused discussion of brain research, understanding treatments, and adolescent addiction. www.hbo.com/addiction.

The National Center on Addiction and Substance Abuse at Columbia University has many summaries of its conferences available through www. casacolumbia.org.National Institute on Drug Abuse (NIDA), National Institute on Alcohol Abuse and Alcoholism. Web sites, articles, and free pamphlets.

WOMEN'S ISSUES

Materials on women's issues from the Stone Center at Wellesley College can be found by e-mailing jbmti@wellesley.edu.

PARENTING

I have found *Systematic Training for Effective Parenting (STEP)* to be a very successful program available in book, workbook, and workshop formats. It covers parenting from childhood through teenage years. Try putting the name into a Web search engine it or call your local Child and Adolescent Mental Health Clinics to obtain other resources for workshops, books, or materials.

Leanne Italie has a number of recent, useful parenting articles available online. Armin Brott is the author of several books on fatherhood and general parenting. He even accepts questions at armin@mrdad.com.

MARRIAGE

Morris, J. 2007. *First comes love; the ever-changing face of marriage.* Cleveland, OH: The Pilgrim Press.